Leadership Dilemmas and Challenges: Reflections and Advice

Leadership Dilemmas and Challenges: Reflections and Advice

(Or, "Why I Do That?")

Michael Zisser

To order additional copies of this book, contact:
Xlibris
1-888-795-4274
www.Xlibris.com
Orders@Xlibris.com
786958

CONTENTS

Prelude

As my two-year old grandchild proceeded to tear up his coloring book, he asked "why I do that?" We found it difficult to suppress our laughter and wondered what other expressions he was quickly picking up as his language and thought processes developed. In a similar vein, as friends read drafts of these interconnected essays, they kept asking me, "why am I writing these and who is the audience?" My grandchild was learning how to think and speak and relate to his adoring audience of loved ones. I'm continuously learning how to think about and express my engagements with the world, as a person and as a professional.

These essays rely on self-reflection and a translation of experiences to understand what I have done, who I am, and what thoughts and advice I might have to offer to fellow practitioners, managers and leaders in the non-profit and public sectors. Adoration is for grandchildren. Adults have to figure out how to confront and address a cascade of challenges, and how to find the forums in which they can openly and honestly communicate.

I have several reasons for writing in the public realm rather than simply keeping a secret diary. The most significant is that there are too few things written today by practitioners in the non-profit or public-sector universe that are intended to be read by current or future practitioners. We have relied on consultants, technical assistance providers, academicians, scholars doing research, to translate, interpret and describe what they have garnered from studying practitioners. The books and articles produced by this collective group convey important facts, insights, managerial typologies, and scenarios for better practice. But they are, by definition, removed from the realities of life on the ground and their inputs are not readily usable at the professional practitioner level.

Do any of us really read any of this stuff? Probably not, unless we're still in school or at a management seminar. Why read when we are too busy doing. There are, however, difficult subjects which need to be identified and analyzed, topics which we know are out there and which have an impact on us every day. We will find the time to read if the writing understands where we are at, what we are experiencing in real time. This book is for and about us. I am both the author, and a member of the potential audience. We should be telling our own stories, and these stories need to be personal.

The second reason for writing in the public realm is that my particular take on the subjects covered comes from my inability to separate the "academic" and "professional" segments of my brain. I was a full-time professor (and Department Chair) of an urban planning program at the graduate level for a number of years. I have continued my teaching career for several decades as an adjunct in several graduate level programs in planning, public administration, and social work. The intellectual pursuit of theories, ideas, models for thinking, has always been a part of my obligations as an educator. For the past thirty years, prior to my "retirement" from full-time work, I served as Chief Executive Officer of a major social services agency in New York City. My years leading University Settlement and The Door through major growth, expansion, innovation, and activism, taught me a few things about how organizations and people help shape the world. Teaching has been one thing; ensuring the success of my organizations has been another. Boundaries have never meant much to me, so every word I have tried to write, every argument I have tried to conceive, derives from a blending of two lives, the inseparability of our complex lives.

Finally, since I am unlikely to ever become a novelist, and even less likely to star in a Broadway musical (lack of both skill and nerve), I must rely on two things I do now possess: both the time and the inclination to be self-reflective in the possible service to others. My wife says my style is more journalistic than scholarly. No footnotes here, no new research. One of my peers says I tend to engage in metaphysical musings. Whatever the motivation I have for this endeavor, I know that people in the non-profit and public sectors want and need to find spaces for reflection. They want to share and converse amongst themselves, with their peers, about what they know to be valuable challenges in their personal and professional lives.

"Why I do that?" My grandchild and I have the same answer. It is in our nature.

Essay One, "Leaving and Arriving," addresses personal and professional transitions, and grew out of a short blog I wrote to share with many of my peers who were contemplating life changes. Perhaps this is better placed at the end of this collection, but I think it serves the purpose of framing many other issues. The blog focused on what I described as practical, or technical issues involved with transition, the immediate concerns one would have and which should not be ignored, minimized, or misunderstood. Responses to the blog suggested that I had ignored the more challenging emotional or psychological aspects of transition. The blog grew into an essay, taking on the complexities of identity and recalibration of values.

Everyone encounters transitions. Everyone faces more or less the same questions needing to be answered or resolved. Everything from "do I have enough resources to live the way I am accustomed," to "what happens with my organization when I can no longer control or protect it," to "what will be my professional legacy as I move forward." More importantly, where and what are the safe forums where these questions can be discussed? The answers are not easily found. This essay outlines many of the inevitable questions; advice, but certainly not universal answers are proffered.

Essay Two, "The Power and Importance of Memory and History," is the most revealing one in this collection and even after constant editing, never escapes two of the principles which have guided my entire work life: (1) there is no separation of one's personal self from one's professional self; and (2) personal memories and history inevitably connect with and directly affect how leaders engage with organizational memories and history. I explore, by using me and a few others as case studies, the extent to which one handles personal memory (e.g. is it suppressed, always on display, irrelevant in its daily impact or oppressively burdensome, etc.)? And how does your connection with memory interact with how others address their own? Our memories and histories shape who we are, but each person is unique in how this plays out. Obvious, yes. Is this phenomenon shared with peers? Rarely if ever.

The stories are endless and almost ubiquitous of how people become managers and leaders of organizations or agencies and act like history began with them. Understanding what came before, let alone paying some respect to those who built what you have inherited, are no longer common attributes of professional character. Needless to say, I argue that without understanding and respect for people, decisions, actions that preceded you, you simply cannot be an effective leader.

Essay Three, "Reconciling Social Justice, Successful Leadership, and a Good Life," pursues what I believe are the vitally important questions of where the principles of social justice are born and how they evolve. Defining "social justice" does not use up much of the mental energy for practitioners whose lives personify social justice values and themes. They are what they believe. But definitional discussions seem to be a preoccupation for academicians, politicians, consultants and others seeking to codify in words what professional live. No specific social justice issue is considered explicitly in this essay. My interest is in origins, motivations, internalized mental constructs for understanding the world and figuring out your role in the world.

The position that one's personal and professional lives cannot be separated is reaffirmed. The importance of a personal code of ethics or moral framework, however hidden or displayed, is emphasized. The sometimes cloudy, imperfect transition that exists between personal and public morality when making important choices or decisions, is presented front and center. And, unavoidably, the argument is made for the relevance of philosophical constructs which influence us every moment of our professional lives – even if more tacit than explicit. Social justice arguments can be made about almost any substantive issue, but in a contemporary society as divisive, as self-reinforcing, as "tribalistic" as the one we're now living, we must be careful to know from whence we came and where we are going.

Essay Four, "Risk and Possible Failure as Key Ingredients for Success," questions the rhetoric espoused by many public and private funders of non-profit agencies in which they espouse respect for and support of programmatic efforts which might result in failure (or incomplete success). My managerial advice is simple. Risk, well managed, is what non-profits should be about. Trying and failing is and should be anticipated and acknowledged, on a scale which does not threaten the survivability of the organization. I have never been able to erase from my mind the Bob Dylan line that "there is no success like failure and failure is no success at all."

There was a time which many remember when foundations, private funders and government agencies sponsored or supported demonstration projects, pilot programs, innovative experimental models, etc. The theory was that such attempts were essential to testing what could work or what would need to be modified to achieve planned success. Those days are gone. I expect arguments are still being made that funders of all stripes still do this sought of thing, i.e. if sufficient backup data is presented, if the program reflects "best practices," if there is a solid case for sustainability once initial funding is ended. There may be exceptions to my argument, but we live primarily in a risk-averse funding universe. Fortunately, there are entrepreneurs in the non-profit and public sectors who understand and pursue risky projects because that is what they do.

Essay Five, "Issues Concerning Risk, or the Subject Frequently Discussed and Rarely Actualized," recognizes the rapidly expanding interest in this subject, and expands on my engagement with the topic reflected in earlier written pieces and one pod cast. As the essay suggests, instruments for assessing risk have been developed in the non-profit and for-profit sectors, and academic institutions - a bit late to the game – have started offering courses (or parts of courses) in an attempt to introduce emerging leaders to the complexities of the subject. My short-hand approach to risk attempts only to display the wide range of managerial questions and potential responses to the questions which will inevitably arise in every organization. Therefore, financial risk, the most popular and sometimes the most important category of risk, is one of only a large number of categories covered.

Equally important, I suggest that even when managers and leaders understand that they must master many aspects of risk analysis, few organizations have the time, resources, managerial culture, self-awareness, or expertise to do the subject justice. Risk assessment tools may be out there to use, and consultants may be available, but the extent of honest, quality, comprehensive assessment is still very limited. The subject, as complicated as it may prove to be, must be mastered. A reminder is provided that risk is what we should be about.

Essay Six, "Thinking About Land Use Ventures for Non-Profits", is the most pragmatic piece of direct advice, and is another expanded version of an earlier blog. I wrote the blog because too many people were asking me to provide a mini-course on how non-profits should engage in complex land use or other strategic planning ventures. The essay summarizes the key steps which any non-profit should consider following. The requests keep coming in, but now I can refer them to this essay.

Frequently, non-profit leaders and their Boards encounter projects or challenges only tangentially related to organizational mission but which could have profound impact on the future of the organization. These could be related to complex land use or real estate transactions, but might also relate to corporate issues like mergers and acquisitions. The important lessons here are clear: the need for leadership direction, the importance of putting together a strong team, the recognition that all numbers are illusory and need constant revision, and so on. We should also recognize the invaluable power of luck and serendipity.

Essay Seven, "The Importance of (Occasionally) Questioning Political Correctness," is a cathartic response to issues which EVERY non-profit manager or leader has and continues to confront. For various reasons, irrespective of their ubiquitous nature, many of these issues are avoided in public discourse. We just can't talk about subjects such as diversity or representation on Boards, giving credit to others, disagreeing and fighting with friends when you're on different sides of the debate, or jeopardizing our professional roles and/or our personal reputations when unpopular positions must be taken. I no longer need to worry about writing on these subjects. I wrote this last essay as an encouragement to others to forget the distinctions between what is considered politically correct or incorrect.

These essays cover very distinct subjects, but they are brought together by the themes which motivated me to write. Leaders and managers in the non-profit and public sectors need to tell their own stories, and not just have them told by observers of our experiences. Each topic is real, alive, and a part of the life of most leaders and managers, even if each appears across a longitudinal professional timeline. Honest and open self-reflection, in which our personal and professional lives must merge and be expressed, is a fundamental principle of effective management.

Essay One

Leaving and Arriving

Being a leader means you will be, by definition, lonely. The higher up you go in leadership positons, the more responsibilities you have, the more risk-laden your decisions, the more profound the implications of your actions, the lonelier it gets. There are fewer people you can honestly and openly talk to with any degree of confidentiality and mutual understanding. Expecting discretion from fellow workers is a risky business at best. Some topics needing to be discussed are considered taboo, difficult to embrace, maybe too personal and revealing. There are few forums which encourage openness and sharing, few opportunities to talk with others who have experienced what you are experiencing or will inevitability experience. And again, few of us are willing or able to write about these things. There are plenty of personal stories out there, plenty of books written by all kinds of people experiencing routine or exceptional lives, but I haven't found many (any) written by former practitioners for their peers or successors.

I have suggested in several forums that leaders need to have dogs (or other pets) to talk to, since pets generally will love you no matter what you say and always seem to agree with your decisions.

And they rarely give back bad advice. Partners may be reasonably reliable, but they have their own lives to worry about or have been listening to your stories for so long they don't want to hear anything more and have little empathy left for worrying about your travails. Even if you have the most empathetic partner in the world, this may not substitute for honest discussions with peers about critical moments in your life plan.

Transitioning from being a leader to being something (or someone) else requires loneliness, isolation, or uncertainty to be overcome, and should be worthy of discussion in the public realm. The "something else" may be called retirement, or the last act at the near-end of your career, or some other dramatically sounding transition signifying that your life is changing forever. There is "the leaving" from someplace, and "the going" towards something, arriving in some new place.

Interlude One: Practical Issues of Leaving

I am reminded of the Paul Simon song, "Fifty Ways to Leave Your Lover," when I think of the many conversations I've had with chief executives or high-level officials in the public and non-profit sectors who have recently retired or are contemplating retirement or later-in-life employment transitions. The retirement/transition issue is ubiquitous these days as the "baby boomer" generation exits the field – or moves to another field - and new people emerge to take over the world we thought was ours to protect forever. Some in our line of business thought the new generation could never replace the one leaving. I feel the opposite. The world demands new talents, new sources of inspiration, new visions, new vocabularies. Our attributes got us this far; now it's time for others to succeed us and own their own accomplishments and mistakes. Our organizations, and ourselves, may sometimes appear to us as being immortal, but they are not and we are not. After countless discussions with friends and peers, both receiving from and dispensing advice to many leaders over many years, I thought I would summarize a few of the most interesting features of transition.

I start with the premise that there are many ways to leave, with no single right way or correct collection of subjects or issues to be addressed. My focus will be only on voluntary transitions. Avoided will be the more dramatic fate felt by many of our friends who have been, rightly or wrongly, gently or not-so-gently, terminated or "disappeared" from their positions of responsibility. My understanding of this issue comes primarily from people who have been with organizations for longer periods of time, not necessarily as founders but certainly as leaders who have been strongly identified with one or a few organizations and where transition is a challenging subject and more impactful than in short-tenured contexts.

*Be planful well in advance of any contemplated transition. Having a plan, a mental map, even if a bit fuzzy or incremental, is critical. This is step one, before you can think about or contemplate other issues which then get subsumed within the plan. The plan must be in your head, and your heart, shared with others or kept secret, firm and strong enough to guide you through what will inevitably happen, and flexible enough to adapt to unknown factors. Since many of us have neither the talent nor inclination to plan or focus in this way, each person must figure out how this exercise becomes real, how the time (real time and psychological time) and safety zone are allowed. Presumably, being planful is what you have being doing throughout your tenure, so this should not entirely be new. As I've learned, even the best thought-out plans get altered almost on a daily basis, but the alterations or changes of course are better accommodated if the main path has been conceived. Like natural disasters, personal disasters are unpredictable and perhaps inevitable, but even "unpredictability" can be incorporated in various scenarios compulsively organized in your head.

*Document (write down) and save as much as you can to share with targeted audiences before you leave or which would be available once you have left. I am not referring here to the routine documents necessitated by your work, like financial reports or a list of key contacts and donors, but the "special" information locked inside your memory and your head. This is a best-management best-practice item often overlooked. What needs to be documented probably differs considerably with each leader and organization, but it is simply not possible to convey verbally and at the last minute the intricacies of your tenure during even the most organized of transitions. The potential readers include your successor, staff, the Board, and possibly certain outside stakeholders. Creating a documents file to pass on does not mean anyone will read it, but it still needs to be available. Your successor(s) may well have a considerably different set of management and leadership skills, therefore increasing the need for documentation of what you knew best. And you might want to look at this stuff later on when you are trying to write a book. Examples? A few would be: program weaknesses you didn't have time to address, or staff who may need to move on but you couldn't pull the trigger, or new deals in the secret stages of development which either need to be dropped or pursued. Do any organizational leaders keep diaries or memoirs, or collections of their letters? I think not.

*Prepare your staff and Board for the transition when the time is right, on a well scheduled and thought out need-to-know basis. The message doesn't have to be that you are leaving, though the message may be obvious to anyone paying attention. Other folks, those staying behind, need to get ready for their own reasons. Preparation can be substantive (e.g. delegating authority or sharing information), or psychological (e.g. hinting about changing personal priorities). The truth does not need to emerge in full-blown messaging. Sometimes slow and steady is better. Timing is everything. Preparation may take months, or longer (but rarely shorter unless you're fired). Do not assume, however, that even the most careful preparation will address everyone's personal issues after you leave, or that the organization will avoid the trauma associated with significant changes in leadership. Preparation is a risk-minimizing strategy.

*Have the necessary substantive conversations with senior staff and the Board which may have been avoided in the past. This is not the same as documentation. Most leaders somehow forget to tell their staff and Boards everything that these key players need to know but never thought to ask or thought they could avoid asking. Did I say forget? Many leaders, myself included, were quite deliberate in keeping too much information to themselves. It's liberating, and scary, to share, especially if you believe that some of your power comes from secrecy. I'm not convinced that social media has made it easier to be transparent in leadership positions; the ground-rules for what is kept inside has merely shifted. Transition means you no longer have any excuses for not sharing.

*Make sure the search firm, if one is being used to fill your position, understands what the real job is about. Search firms generally have set in their minds the standard definitions for what top leaders are about and the characteristics or qualifications which are needed, but these are frequently too naïve and simplistic. These packaged job descriptions are obvious and somewhat uninstructive. The sustainability of many search firms is based on the model of creating a stable of applicants for future positions, hoping that whomever they place will be available for other placements somewhere in the future. **Write your own job description** to give to the Board, separate from and in addition to the package being put together by the search firm. If no search firm is being used, make sure your Board knows what the job involves. This is not the job you were doing, but the job which needs to be done when you leave. Insightful job descriptions are not about the skill sets or experiences required, but about the personality traits necessary for survival and success. In the job-description I wrote for my Board, and shared with a few others, I had some of the following characteristics: have a sense of humor; not be susceptible to ulcers from too much stress; understand that all "s…" rises to the top; be willing to risk failure; and, of course, my favorite, know whether you would prefer to be feared or loved. The real questions to be asked of prospective applicants are exactly the ones Human Resources people will tell you are either illegal or inappropriate.

*Take care of as many of your leftover unfinished projects as you can, to the greatest extent possible. The "extent" may be minimal, and probably should be targeted to the items which are suggested by senior management who are staying, but the need to leave as clean a slate as possible is unavoidable. The primary goal here is to lessen (but certainly not to remove, which would be impossible) the baggage left behind for others to address. Since many of the projects under the domain of top leaders involve longitudinal time lines, leaving a relatively clean desk is another critical timing decision. Successors always have the right to ignore or minimize projects which they inherit as they pursue their own directions. Successors will also have the challenge of inventing their own initiatives…and their own timelines.

*Do not start longer-term projects which will transcend the timeline you have established for your transition. New projects may be tempting, and the pursuit of them may be in your blood, but acting on them would not be wise. This point should go into effect early in the planning stage. Not starting leadership-driven projects is an easy way of signaling that you may have transition on your mind. The extent to which signaling is picked up by others would be an interesting test for those other leaders in the organization who will be staying. This was one of the more difficult challenges for me to master, since my management style drove me to invent new longer-term projects on a routine basis. Stopping this internal drive has carried over to my retirement. The flip side of this suggestion is to start a number of new things that you believe the organization should pursue, and carry them forward enough so that your successor has to finish the job. You may be happy with this, your successor won't, and the organization may have a bit of a problem.

*Think (however fluid) about your future. A reminder again to be planful! The most consistent advice I received from others when I was thinking about retirement was to make no big plans or big decisions ahead of time, even if you have a well thought out plan. Most folks said, "make no new commitments for at least a year," which seems like good advice for most of us, unless you're over worried about the "being invisible" thing (see below). There should be no rush. Instead, prepare for uncertainty, prepare for the unknown, and prepare for choices never envisioned. These are not contradictory statements. Generalizations here don't work since each of our life situations is different, but when transitioning, we all face some of the same questions about the future. The truth is, now that I am entering my third year of "retirement," I have been reexamining this one-year hiatus recommendation and asking myself if I was too rigid in adherence to the rule or in not allowing for exceptions.

*Figure out the money thing ahead of time. Many of my peers experiencing transitions have said to me that they either screwed up or misunderstood the financial separation/transition they experienced or incorrectly anticipated what they would need to live on in a hoped-for life style. Unfortunately, this fact is true not just for leaders, but for many others. Professional help may be needed here. I've suggested to executives that their Boards hire compensation firms to do the necessary research and generate viable options for consideration. Budgeting your own life could be much harder than managing organizational finances, unless perhaps you apply the same rules to both contexts. I would guess that the majority of non-profit leaders, and their Boards, do not spend sufficient time and resources on figuring out the best financial transition plan, or are even aware of the legal mechanisms available in the non-profit field. It's almost as if our social justice value systems prevent us from thinking selfishly about our financial security. Get over it. No one retires so they can worry every morning about paying bills or going out for dinner or having to sell their homes and moving to a lower tax state. The stock market goes up and down. Thinking about money, make sure to work out your deal (if any) before you leave. Boards are likely to stop loving you once you're out of sight.

*Don't think you will become a completely different person after transition. Transition is not the same as being reborn with a new persona. You're always the same old person. Don't think the way you leave will be different than the way you stayed, i.e. management styles and personal styles don't change last minute. Deciding to leave does not mean that all of a sudden you become more wise or insightful or effective as a leader, or as a person.

*Understand that the place you are leaving is no longer yours and has a future existence without you. People will start thinking about themselves and their futures (even if they may miss you) the moment they know transition is about to occur. Such is human nature. Some will stay, others will go, some will be happy, others sad, and there's not much you can or should do about any of this. Whatever the world thinks you did right or wrong will be the final word, at least for a while. Everything is a matter of perception, myths, facts (or alternate facts), reputation, deserved or not. Your legacy will be written and enshrined…or buried… by others.

Memory will shape and define the past, as well it should. And, over time, the above items become less important…if you remember them at all. At any rate, **Practical** issues are easier to contemplate than the next group of issues.

Interlude Two: Emotional and Psychological Factors in Leaving

To what extent is your **identity** mostly or completely tied to your professional persona? Or is your **identity** defined in some other manner, less dependent on the professional or leadership roles you have occupied for much of your life? This is one exploration I'm not sure I can undertake on behalf of others, because it is so idiosyncratic. Identity is by definition so profoundly personal, that even finding a forum for sharing is difficult to imagine. All **Practical Issues** raised above are obviously influenced by where you sit on the identity spectrum, but the issues described below more directly affect the identity concern since they are more personal. I will try to outline a few thoughts which might help shape this discussion.

The central theme is that we are continuously experiencing a rearrangement or recalibration of our values. This process, with enormously important implications, happens throughout our lives, and certainly happens at different stages of our leadership and managerial evolution. Decisions I made closer to the end of my career were based on a very different balancing of relevant facts and experiences and considerations than when I was younger. This should come as no surprise to anyone who feels wiser or more trusting in one's "judgment" the older one gets. The same rules apply at key points of transition: the weighting of values, the measuring of key objectives, understanding the importance of consequences (positive and negative) of choices made.

*Becoming Invisible. In my realm of experiences, the most commonly heard phenomenon resulting from transition, and especially the retirement (by any definition) version of transition, is that suddenly you become invisible to the world in which you once thrived. You have been what your title says you have been, with all that the title implies. Then you're not. This may be simultaneously correlated with becoming older, a different but related form of invisibility. How is this manifested in real-world terms? You're no longer invited to be at the table; people don't call you anymore; you get fewer emails or texts; you're taken off distribution lists; invitations to panels and workshops diminish; no one wants your advice or opinion; other people seem to have emerged with their

own voices while yours vanishes; board memberships decline or are withdrawn; a new generation claims your positions on issues once important to you. Other names, other voices, other leaders, seem to have taken your place. When I've discussed this list of possible examples of invisibility with others, women almost uniformly say things are worse for them for a variety of reasons, but I can only write my story.

Is becoming invisible inevitable with transition? Can this be countered if becoming invisible frightens you too much? Yes, to some extent. There are innumerable ways to stay connected, to stay relevant, but they may require effort, persistence and diligence, intentionality. Some folks become consultants, independently or working with others. Some take on new jobs with new responsibilities, hopefully less demanding and pressured than previous roles. Some continue to attend fund raising events to socialize and network, speak at or attend conferences, stay on Boards or join new Boards, become visiting faculty members or mentors, and (in my case) enjoy a plethora of breakfasts and lunches with friends and peers where the conversation drifts back and forth between personal matters and the sharing of professional advice. Here's to the former leaders who lunch!

For each force that drives you towards invisibility, there is a possible equal and opposite force keeping you engaged in the issues and with the people still important to your identity. I can still envision the fate of more than one of my peers who retired and then expected to be immediately called to serve as a paid consultant given their reputations and expertise. No calls materialized. A bit sad. What could have happened? Have you become invisible because without your role you are irrelevant with nothing to offer?

But I've witnessed many more positive stories, about how busy folks became after their so-called retirement, busy with the multitude of things they want to do or are asked to do. Until the day arrives, it may be difficult to know what story will play out.

I would guess that for many there is a transition to the transition, i.e. the process of staying visible goes on for a while, with good days and bad days. The first year after transition is certainly different than the following years, and don't forget the age thing which somehow keeps moving forward. Being invisible is not good for one's self-identity if a particular definition of visibility is considered a virtue. Or you could no longer care to any great extent about being visible in the old manner, and instead "recalibrate" and celebrate the new ordering of values, the new and even better arranging of what's important and why. All the negatives or worries I have mentioned may simply become unimportant, or less important to you at this stage in life. There is something to be said for closing a chapter and believing that the next chapter is not directly related to one's previous life. I think that's why someone invented golf (which I do not play), or fishing (which I also do not do), or moving to a "retirement" state or country where hurricanes come with some frequency (which I have not done), or going on a succession of cruises (which I will never do), or even taking one or more long vacations (which never fit our family schedule).

Or on a more affirmative note from my vantage point, one can spend much more time with children or grandchildren (which I am now doing!!!), or attempt writing (which I am now trying to do), or learning how to handle a riding lawn mower (which I love), or doing the lunch thing (which is wonderful though you have to watch your diet), or going to the gym (which is fine for me when I keep away from the TVs set on CNN or FOX or the buying channels), or volunteering to work on behalf of people or organizations similar or quite different from those you were associated with in the past. In other words, **there is no such thing as becoming invisible once you decide that your entire identity is not tied to the position you are leaving or once held.** Settling in to a new life style may take some time and not be so easy, but in fact this is what people do with great success.

My friends and peers know I would not have retired exactly when I did if my older daughter had not given birth to my first grandchild. In my last six months of employment, when my retirement date had been set, I cut back to four days a week so I could be the "nanny" on Fridays. I've performed this role ever since, from the time my grandson was three months old. Not everyone gets to have this incredibly rewarding identity, and this is certainly not the only opportunity out there. But this special experience shapes **"why I do that."**

*Separation Anxiety. Leaving the job is one thing. Leaving relationships is quite another, and in most situations much more difficult. Even though I was accused of not always being sensitive enough in certain work relationship situations, many people said I suffered from separation anxiety when employees with whom I was close left the organization. While there are many benefits to no longer having the burdens and responsibilities of leadership, and perhaps many benefits to no longer having to participate in professional relationships which had little personal value for you, the loss of true relationships can be challenging and difficult to replace. This loss happens on the job, and during transition. For those who stay a long time in leadership positions, the likelihood of loss is inevitable and oftentimes repeated across your tenure. I never resolved this issue when working, and probably buried much of my feelings. I did try to recognize the impact of addressing this form of anxiety, and did try to make the phenomenon as public as possible, either through humor or serious contemplation. Many of my "kids," those who grew up as professionals under my tenure, are doing good things and trying to change the world.

I continue to see a few of my former Board members and staff who I consider to be friends. I continue to see peers who I consider to be friends. I have also, on a somewhat regular basis, deleted names from my Contact List because there is little likelihood I will ever need to talk to them again. Some of these deletions were mistakes, however, and I have needed to return them to the List when former relationships reappeared with new meaning!

One of the more fascinating aspects of leaving a role, is the realization that many people may have related to you not because of who you are (were), but because of what you had to offer them. No surprise here. The value of friendship has many points on the spectrum. For several months after my retirement, I kept a mental list of people I expected would contact me because of the positive role I had played in their lives. Time went by, many contacts from the list never materialized. Deleting their names has been easy.

*Your Baby Belongs to Someone Else. I cried when we dropped our kids off at college and drove home without them. I cried at each of my daughter's weddings, noting in my "father" speeches that I had now been pushed down the rung as their husbands replaced me as (presumably) the number one male in their lives. I did NOT cry when I decided to retire, nor did I cry at any of the events which followed that decision, for reasons which I'm not quite sure I understand. A whole year passed before I put the flash drive in my computer which contained all the "good-bye" speeches (most of them quite funny) from peers and those who worked for me at one time or another. I know that many of my friends were far more emotional than me when they "retired," who did cry or tear up for reasons consistent with who they are and how they acted in their roles.

I will suggest a few reasons why giving up one's baby varies amongst us, while trying to avoid any comparison with children leaving home and growing up. First, organizations have lives which transcend yours. This fact must be understood at the deepest possible level. Except in "founders" situations, the organization existed before you and will exist after you. Even with founders, the hope and expectation is that the organization can live without you once you have left. **You are, de facto, always a steward and not an owner or parent.** You play your role for as long as you want or can, and then your role is over. This view is connected to my belief that institutions have histories and trajectories that are separate from and more powerful over time than individuals. Sooner or later, your baby belongs to someone else, as it belonged to someone else before you came along. (Note: the exact opposite is true with your children, or with your parents. For better or worse, they are always yours; there is no before, and no after.)

Controversial to some, because it is subject to interpretation, is the premise that organizations over time take on a bit of the "personality" of their leader(s), which gets absorbed into the personalities which have existed before. I don't mean to suggest that bureaucracies are completely subject to personalities, but would argue that leadership can greatly influence the culture and style of organizational life. In the same way that you have shaped your organization, you must understand that someone else will inevitably shape it differently in the future. This is the right, and the obligation, of new leaders, especially those who plan on sticking around.

*Where Do You Fit in History? I began this book by believing that respecting memory and history is not necessarily our professional strong point unless your organization is lucky enough to have people who care about memory and history. Non-profit leaders do not exist in an environment where leaders become a recognized part of American history, immortalized in texts or movies, such as Jane Adams in the settlement house universe (though Hull House is no longer with us). They may become part of a more focused history known and honored by interested parties, but we're generally not in the "famous" category. I'm trying to remember the last time a non-profit leader got much of a write-up in the New York Times obituary section, or when a book written by a non-profit leader became part of the organizational theory canon. Being remembered and having an identity are part of the same subject, either to be worried about or not. Hopefully, long after you have transitioned out of your leadership position, your successors (and many of your former staff) will remember you and what you achieved .and, quite possibly what you did wrong. Plaques at some point just become background décor. Maybe you'll have a space named after you, though in future years, people may say, "who was that?"

Brief Digression: Can an Organization Transcend Its Reputation and Culture Even When Everything Changes?

Many years ago, I wrote a short piece on how organizational culture sometimes lives in the walls, is a part of an environment which cannot be exorcised even if you replace the walls and all the inhabitants. Culture is as pervasive as a permanent bureaucracy, but much harder to discern. Of course, I was partly wrong. Culture does change, but slowly, like the permanent bureaucracy. The measuring stick may be hard to define, and the change can be imperceptible. For example, organizations today with new younger staff frequently have a better understanding of the need for data and the required quantitative analysis for quality control or performance measurement. Almost everyone on staff in 2018 understands the range and impact of social media, reserved not too long ago for members of the development department. Things move faster these days….and people change jobs even faster, all of which has an impact on the stability of organizational culture. Management styles may be more enlightened, perhaps a bit more sensitive to certain "human" needs. Remodeling space, redoing tag lines, changing "brand" recognition by changing the name of the organization, are all now part of the lexicon. Sexual harassment is better understood and thankfully more universally condemned. But do any of these factors substantially change culture, or are they simply ways of keeping busy and acting like you're doing something useful. Mostly, only time will tell, but if my comments on memory still hold, time may make only a slight difference.

Earning and keeping an organization's reputation is different, more challenging and less under your control. Reputations are built on years of quality work, years of good press, an endless library of stories and oral histories conveyed through the years by loving and loyal long-tenured staff. Since reputations are also built on the opinions of outsiders, the perception of good work, the belief in great stories, and the acceptance of positive messaging all play roles. And all this can be wrecked in an instant, harmed or destroyed with short notice, exposing vulnerabilities you never imagined.

Brief Digression: Thoughts on the Differences Between Luck and Skill in Achieving Success

One of my clearest memories of a Board member's comments about a real estate deal I was pursuing on behalf of the organization, was something like "better to be lucky than smart." In other words, dumb luck frequently outweighs talent. I would rather have used the word "serendipity," or the expression "be at the right place at the right time," or the more sanguine thought that luck or good fortune is what you make of it when it happens. For better or worse, I may be remembered more for a few real estate transactions than for the more important policy and program issues I focused on in my long tenured leadership position. Were skills required in making any of these deals a success? Certainly, mostly focused on knowing which critically important experts were needed at every step in the transaction.

My primary skill, however, was having the patience to work through multi-year processes which are standard in land use transactions or significant programmatic expansions. But if the local zoning code had not "invented" the concept of air-rights, or a struggling non-profit with a great facility as an asset had not called upon us to rescue their operations, had not the market made some land we owned far more valuable than anyone expected it to be, or had the government decided not to substantially increase public funding for specific programs, than patience and expertise would not have been sufficient for success. The point is – especially when considering identity and place in history – that many of the variables which have shaped our success were beyond our control, were elements in the larger political, economic and policy universe, and were out there for us to either take advantage of or miss. This is not an argument for humility. There are differences between successful and unsuccessful leaders, those capable of taking advantage of the moments in time when goals can be achieved.

Essay Two

The Power and Importance
of Memory and History

No one performs in any role within a personal or organizational vacuum. Memory and history guide and help define individual actions and style as they simultaneously affect organizational behavior and evolution. **The essential value of understanding the burdens and wisdom of personal and organizational memory and history is the first lesson I can offer to prospective and current leaders in any field.** As obvious as this lesson might appear here on paper, it is infrequently witnessed in practice, to the inevitable detriment of professional accomplishment and the achievement of organizational goals.

I can't remember anything that happened to me before the age of eight, the year my mother died, the only exceptions being random and infrequent visual or auditory flashes. My dreams vanish the moment I wake up, so they don't count as valid memories. The flashes mostly connect to other traumatic childhood events. Only a few pictures remain, which trigger no strong emotional or sensate responses, and no family members are around anymore to fill in the stories or facts.

Given all I have learned or know about early childhood (brain) development, what the impact of stress can have on emotional development, this vacuum of memories fascinates me. Somehow, I got formed, but I don't know how. Does this worry me, these many decades later? Other dramatic personal events which occurred later in life are much clearer in my head, some lodged so permanently that they surface even now on a regular basis, many in precise moment by moment detail, inescapable, having obvious influence. Most of these events relate to failed or incomplete relationships. Many of these events were wonderful, especially witnessing the birth of my two daughters. Discovering what's buried deep down, or revisiting even inescapable events or feelings does not now seem to be worth the price or time demands of therapy, and I'm not convinced that further discovery or introspection would be helpful. I'll leave these memories to an active though occasionally stressful dream life, forgotten, as I noted, at the moment of awakening. And yet, I am profoundly aware that memories hidden or visible affect every move I make.

I am now more interested in what this lack of memory, or this selective filtered memory, this lack of understanding of important early influences and relationships, or occasional surfacing of influences and relationships, has meant to how I function as an adult in my personal life and how I have performed as a non-profit manager. How have I formed and maintained relationships, with friends and families and peers; how have I made critical on-the-job decisions in a complex managerial universe; how have I presented myself to the world and how have I been perceived? There are moments when I have had to look across the table trying to discern how other people were formed by their pasts, how their lives defined the way they performed their jobs, how our lives interconnected, were similar or vastly different, in strange but powerful ways. **There is no separation of personal stories from professional life.**

Somehow, I learned to bury or erase or block parts of the past, successfully suppressing or minimizing their importance in my daily waking life. Suffocating memory has been either a deliberate or tacit strategy, without conscious consent and apparently not explicitly detrimental to my well-being. This has meant, in practice, that past events, even sometimes recent past events, lose explicit value or relevance or influence, while others permeate my thoughts in sometimes insidious ways. There's minimal baggage to interfere with my actions. Hurts, or slights or criticisms are quickly forgotten. Similarly, compliments or achievements or success are noted and then get filed where I don't have to think about them. Once you get used to the repression mode of behavior, certain life patterns prevail.

For sure, what I have written above contradicts my public advocacy for the power of memory and history in creating and sustaining organizational culture and identity. Equally contradictory is the reality that the way I react to the world connects all too powerfully with whatever recollections of my past I can dredge up at key moments. My professional life has been strongly based on the belief in and the power of memory, traditions, history....and an equally strong counter-belief that very few professionals with whom I've interacted over the years care about history or any form of inquiry that requires understanding what came before yesterday (buried or hidden in memory).

On a very pragmatic level, I have interacted with Board members and managerial leaders, people in the public sector, and representatives from the philanthropic community, who respect and try to understand the history of their organizations or their place in a larger organizational universe. And I have interacted with many who do not care, or show minimal interest, or even acknowledge that they are missing something. I have interacted with too many people who still believe they can separate who they are or where they came from in the performance of their professional roles. My central theme here is that in one's personal life, and in one's professional life, there is no avoidance of history, of memory, no matter how successful we are at suppression or skilled at ignoring yesterday(s).

I will use a few stories from my work/life to argue the principle that there is no separation of personal and professional selves. The stories are sometimes directly literal, and sometimes illustrative of combined experiences. These stories are mine, as they could be yours, and have not been tempered by third-party translations. I chose not to ask permission of the people "hidden" in these stories, knowing some would be pleased with my real or based-on-real characterizations and some would be upset, especially if they were identifiable. But I must write; it is my new life. Anyone could do the same, but unfortunately there are few professionals in the non-profit sector who have chosen to express themselves in writing. This is a mostly true set of stories.

Interlude: Story 1, or Different Ways to Remember

Shortly after I retired, I met with one of my former staff members with whom I shared a very good and close professional relationship. She worked for me for many years, a large portion of her professional life. She had also recently retired; or not so much retired as pursuing a new professional direction to recharge her energy and her interests. I had an agenda to pursue in our meeting, held over cappuccinos in a Greenwich Village restaurant: to ask her to stop interfering with how her successor and her former subordinates were dealing with challenging staff and program issues. She said she would honor my request (more or less, depending on circumstances!), but then quickly moved beyond my concerns and spent almost two hours recalling the long list of things about which she was still angry with me, irrespective of our positive relationship. She hadn't forgotten or suppressed these issues. They had been held closely in her consciousness, close to the surface, as important to her the day we spoke as when they occurred, in many cases years ago.

I could hardly remember most of the issues, and to the extent I did remember them, I did not feel as if my ongoing behavior had in any way been affected. Or maybe they did affect me and I didn't know it. These stories evidently shaped every moment of her working life…and afterwards. I hadn't told her about my retirement prior to the public announcement; I hadn't discussed with her the elevation of one of her peers to a more senior management position; I hadn't arranged (to the extent I could) for one of her key people to replace her when she left the organization; and so on. Her way of dealing with these "hurts" regarding my leadership was to look inwards and figure out how to do her job as well as possible – which she did beautifully – accommodating rather than suppressing memory.

Perhaps we got along because our styles were so different, because our managerial instincts played well against and with each other. But what is important to me now is that we understood who we were and why we were this way. Even as I sat there (two cappuccinos later) fascinated by her memories, I somewhat gently made clear that I wasn't at all sorry about my actions when confronted and surprised by their impact on a person so close to me. A follow-up lunch several months later, at a different coffee shop, focused on the same conversation. Her memory was still vivid, my memory even fuzzier, while we were both well into our new lives.

This dynamic between me and former staff members has surfaced several times in the past year or two, sometimes over coffee, sometimes with a full lunch, sometimes just by email to soften the impact. If I were less secure at this stage in my life, I might have thought, "...so they didn't really love me." If her memories and feelings and those of hundreds of other staff had consciously stayed in my head, had continuously affected my performance because they were alive, I would have been immobilized and incapable of moving forward free of endless psychological shackles. But at the same time, my head was (is) filled with a vast array of information, facts, stories, about the substantive program or administrative fields and areas of expertise which obviously were having an impact on my life and how I performed my leadership responsibilities. My head was (is) filled with an understanding of what leadership and management requires of all of us in such positions of authority. My head was (is) always filled with memories of relationships, positive and negative.

Decisions were never abstractions; they were rooted in experiences, some of which caused pain, others satisfaction. I was never acting in a vacuum when addressing the multitude of issues presented by running large scale programs or addressing personal matters. Knowing what has worked, what has failed, what people have written or experienced, seems to me an indisputable attribute, and not simply to avoid repeating history. Wisdom comes from understanding, and understanding relies on the past, present, and future. Much of our work may be immediate, in the present, when making decisions which have impact on people, programs, and institutions. The true measure of rightness or wrongness in decision making, however, requires a longitudinal assessment which we may or may not be around to witness or understand.

Now I am assuming that to the extent I communicate with former employees of mine, their "affection" for me may well become balanced or tempered by the issues they might have had with my managerial style or the many decisions I made. Does this bother me? Not in the least. My affection for people depends on many factors, and has never been dependent on selective memory. And let's not forget, I might as easily have been wrong in my decisions, ineffective or inappropriate in some of these relationships, not cognizant of key historical facts or events, while I was serving as an organizational leader. Others get to tell their own stories. Every leader, at every level, processes his or her relationships with fellow workers. There may be no one right way to relate, but understanding how you do relate seems to be essential.

Recently, an email came from another person who worked for me for many years, after I sent a note congratulating her on earning a wonderful new high level non-profit position. She writes: "Your words mean so much. I said it before and I'll say it again, I carry your brutally honest words to heart to this day." I've chosen not to ask her what she meant by using the term "brutally."

Interlude: Story 2, History Begins When You Walk in the Door

This story is about many people, a rather large percentage of people I've known who are (or were) relatively new to their positions in top non-profit or public-sector institutions. Originally, it was about one person, currently working at an organization I know well, but as I discussed the subject with friends and peers, I realized a more generalized approach would be more appropriate, and more accurate. For too many people who manage or lead organizations, the history of the organizations began the day they arrived. When people make this claim or act in this way, it is partly meant (I must assume) as a humorous statement not to be taken literally, and partly as a serious personal perspective on the value of history or tradition or whatever happened in the organization's past. Certainly, most leaders know about the history of the organizations and agencies they are joining, either from past professional experiences or exposure, or general knowledge of the field. Some may even have read many of the key documents detailing that history, recognizing the importance, to some extent, of what happened before, and respecting some of the people who created that history.

Having an operating frame of reference is critically important, and no frame of reference exists outside of time. For any new leader, to what extent does memory or history influence or affect future behavior? What happens when, in effect, there is no acknowledgement or recognition of critically important memories or historical facts/decisions, to burden one's perspectives on today or tomorrow? Prior relationships, events, decisions may be important, but only up to a point. They could be recognized, acknowledged, respected, ignored, set aside, minimized, or associated with any other appropriate negative verb, up to a point. This is not, as I hinted earlier, an unusual quality in our field, the quality of denying or minimizing memory and history. To the contrary, it is ubiquitous, the rule rather than the exception

In its extreme form, denying history and memory comes with a need to demonize the past, not only to forget but to explicitly reject past acts of others. I've seen this phenomenon most frequently when leadership in government positions changes, usually with new administrations, but it also happens routinely in the non-profit world. I'm not sure I can come up with a reasonable rationalization for what amounts to an unfortunate transitional "rule" practiced by too many people. Almost by definition, what others accomplished before you must be minimized, made less important, irrespective of worth.

Change the names of policies you don't like and either re-name or bury them. Forbid referring to them as positive influences in staff meetings or in the designs of new policies. Unless a framed picture is required of past leaders to be hung on the conference room wall, let's pretend they have been disappeared from our memories. Overstated? Perhaps, but ask anyone now in a powerful leadership position at any level of government, or the leaders of almost all non-profit sector organizations, if what I suggest has any truth to it. The two best explanations for this behavior, which were told to me by a former high ranking elected government official, is that people are driven by insecurity and the need for revenge.

I've known many excellent leaders who either ignore the past or occasionally demonize those who came before, so I can't definitively argue that anyone suffers because of a de facto new "start date" for the organization. I would argue, however, that the long-term stability and strength of the organization depends on a blurring of the lines between one generation of leaders and the next, and understanding the power of a continuum of facts, decisions, events, styles. History cannot be avoided. Memories (and their value) are not automatically transferred from one generation of leaders to another. Intentionality is required. Stuff happened before, and will happen afterwards. Memories and an understanding of history must be passed on, accepted, internalized, assimilated into one's own state of consciousness.

The danger of carrying too much memory is that it could be a trap for avoiding creative, innovative, even ground- breaking actions critical to the organization's future. We frequently hear, as excuses for non-action, "there's no such thing as a new idea," "been there done that," "we've tried and failed/succeeded before," "there's nothing new under the sun" – suggesting an easily accessible language for over-emphasizing the importance or downside of reacting to history negatively or positively. I would hate to overstate my argument. But perhaps I'm more of an academic traditionalist, or elitist, remembering a line from a song I can't remember (typically), something like "you ain't done nothing that hasn't been done before." This perspective, however, can never be used as a way to avoid action.

I'm not sure I could come up with a magical formula for how much the past should influence the present or the future; in any case, the formula might well depend on how long people stay in their positions or within their organizations. Short-termers need worry less about history, because they will occupy such a small segment on the organizational time line; and long-termers eventually create their own narratives, highlighting what they prefer and hiding what they wish to be hidden. This is, to be clear, not about **nostalgia**, a word with negative connotations when it limits moving forward. The freedom to move forward successfully can only be sharpened when the past has its rightful place in one's thoughts.

Brief Digression: There Are No More Classics

A few years back, when I was an adjunct faculty member teaching in a different prestigious graduate management program than where I am now, I would oftentimes joke with my students that the program insisted that all required readings had to have been written no further back than the past five years. Okay, I was not joking. I did study the syllabi from other classes, and from people who had taught the class I was doing in prior years. Lo and behold, my theory held! There was no intellectual literary history evident in the program. Maybe the rationale was that new authors had to be acknowledged and utilized or academic scholarship would come to a halt. Or maybe professors believed that something dramatically new had been discovered for which the world was waiting breathlessly.

Or maybe there is no such thing as the "great books" concept in some graduate programs. Or maybe faculty thought students would be bored by authors or writings which preceded their births or written in a style with complex sentence structures. I don't know how many times I have had to assert that there have been hundreds of variations on what some called "the strategic planning process," each variation with a new name, a presumably new lens with which to view the world. They are, essentially, all the same. Only the authors and publication dates change.

Unfortunately, I never outgrew my University of Chicago undergraduate bias towards a great books theory of obtaining common knowledge, and wondered why no "classics" (updated every so often to keep everyone somewhat honest) were taught in my course or in most other courses. Was there no history, no memory, to be shared between professors and students? Was there no collective canon of written wisdom which, to some extent, new people in the field should be exposed? This became the starting place for my requiring students to read (sections of) The Prince by Machiavelli, and selected excerpts from The Federalist Papers (always #10 and #51), maybe one or two pieces from Peter Drucker or Herbert Simon or Max Weber, maybe even something by Kafka, or whomever. And I outlawed all of what I called "pop-management" books, some of which routinely made it on to The New York Times bestseller list but are primarily derivative. I suggested to students that they look at the bibliographies of books which popularize more complex ideas, and to go read the "original" texts.

I now teach in a program where some faculty are hesitant to ask students to do too much reading, and certainly neither acknowledge nor assign many "classics", using any definition of what constitutes a classic. The primary reason for this position is the belief that students (even graduate students) have neither been trained nor disciplined to read critically (except in 140 characters or less). Again, as a traditionalist or elitist, I would argue that if you can't read, you can't speak. And if you can't write in reasonably complex sentence structures, you can't develop sound arguments, and therefore cannot be a strong leader. When I shared this Great Books dilemma with some of my fellow teachers, a few presented a different problem: professors who never change their reading lists for whatever reasons, and are therefore presenting students with "stale" requirements. I believe this issue has been addressed by those who believe in having some classics required of an educated student by updating the canon on a regular basis, letting new books on to the list and even occasionally making others recommended rather than required.

Brief Digression: Advice on Starting a New Job

This essay is not an accounting of my recent professional life, but two additional aspects of how memory and history play out in real life are worth noting as potential advice for others. In the first few months of my beginning work at University Settlement, and a decade later in the first few months of the Settlement's taking responsibility for The Door, I utilized a very simple though time consuming practice. I devoured everything I could read about the history of the organization (thousands of pages from the files), the history of the fields I was entering (the world of settlement houses in the first place, and later the world of youth development for at risk young adults), and the political context in which the organizations operated (including an understanding of the role of government and philanthropy in the ongoing success of the organizations). I even read a countless array of proposals submitted to foundations (some accepted, others not) and samples of approved government sponsored contracts. Why? I just needed to know what happened before me, with no interest in praising or demonizing those who formally did the work.

In the community of scholarly writing, this would be considered basic essential background research undertaken before one explores a specific topic of choice. Know what's been written and documented, and the reasons why! I even read some of the footnotes. Steep yourself in history (knowing the selectivity of how history gets documented), and try to uncover what the memories of others have to teach you about the past and future. And to be fair and transparent, I was helped by there being a rich history of the settlement movement, some of which prematurely declared the end of the movement, and an actual history of University Settlement's first hundred years (1886-1986) written by the historian Jeff Scheuer who also served for a time as a Board member. A few years back, I added to this organizational history by writing a sequel to Jeff's Legacy of Light, by chronicling the story of the Settlement's next twenty-five years. Someone else will have to document years 126-150.

For me, teaching responsibilities include conveying to a possible new generation of non-profit leaders the history of the field they are entering. This responsibility has become more challenging as the demands of being a leader go well beyond the knowledge contained in any one discipline, e.g. social work or public administration, and must include the several disciplines required for leadership. One of the graduate courses I have taught the past few years was in a newly developed program which attempts to combine the core elements of non-profit business management with the core elements of a social work/social justice mindset. From my perspective, this is exactly what needs to happen at the graduate level, creating cross disciplinary degrees, but the challenge of conveying to students the roots of those two disciplines has not been easy. Can a student be expected to read the "classics" in business, management, organizational psychology, social work, community building, etc., all in one degree program? Obviously not, so the concept and challenges of "life-long" learning frequently arises.

The second piece of advice concerns the personal dilemma of remembering who you were at different stages in your own career. I can't count the multitude of times I was asked about how or why I did things earlier in my professional life which led to the current status of the organizations from which I recently retired. For some reason, people interpreted today's understanding of the organizations as constant over time. Or they assumed I was the same person today as I was decades ago regarding expertise, wisdom, or whatever terms people would apply to me, positive or negative. Quite obviously I had grown older and hopefully learned something along the way. So back to memory and history. Since you can only be who you are at the moment, creating a record of what you did or who you were could be helpful. Documentation is helpful. Having a reliable, and somewhat objective memory is also helpful, especially if you acknowledge that you may not have always been right when you were younger. Files (on paper or in the cloud) are essential for personal and historical reasons. Each new generation will have to discover its own way of discovering history, but there must be something to discover.

The subjects of memory and use of history are deep complex subjects, and I don't pretend that what I write here adds to the scholarly discipline. Even the inter-mixing of the terms "memory" and "history" could make me a suspect interpreter of important ideas. My goal is, however, much simpler. **Top leaders and managers in the non-profit arena are in the business of exercising their judgment, making decisions large and small on a daily and longer-term basis. They need to know their organizations, the fields in which they operate, the contexts which shape their worlds. They need to believe in the necessity and power of history, and they need to understand that memory can't be erased or ignored. Ignorance or lack of curiosity is no defense against anything.**

Essay Three

Reconciling Social Justice, Successful Leadership and a Good Life

Social Justice as a Framework for Managerial Action

Not everyone needs an applied conceptual framework for envisioning social justice, so to a large extent this essay is targeted to a self-selected audience of people (or believers). Not everyone can articulate the conceptual framework in which they operate, though it is buried in there somewhere. People in the human services, or public administration or management, or educational fields, or any public service role, might find value here. Their beliefs may be clear, but they may not be sure how they apply to current or future employment.

What follows are a few guiding structural management principles which provide a conceptual framework for social justice, simple enough that they might easily apply in real-world contexts. Each one of these could come with a lengthy how-to bibliography, a depth of understanding well beyond my intentions in this essay. Each of these derives directly from a real-world context.

First, there should be no major differences between your sense of private morality and your applied understanding of professional morality. Presumably, the former develops long before you get to implement the second. I say "major" because there will inevitably be moments when your managerial behavior may have to vary from what you might do in a personal situation. In one's personal life, there are more likely to be absolutes with strict prohibitions which might not hold in professional settings, e.g. translations of the "shalt nots" of the Ten Commandments. There are likely to be affirmative qualities in how you conduct your life but not necessarily your job, e.g. tithing for charity, volunteering for causes you admire or respect, loving thy neighbors, being kind and caring and thoughtful in relating to others.

They emerge from how and where you were raised, how you were educated, what constitutes your cultural, religious or social background. Private morality is not only about good and bad, right and wrong, virtue or vice, duties and rights. It is also about intentionality, choice, deep understanding of who you are, acceptance of responsibilities which lead to making moral decisions and assessments oftentimes on a daily basis, and defining goodness or badness as they apply to actions or decisions that are a projection of character. Private morality structures the way we live, defines the way we see ourselves as individuals and members of a community. The dilemma comes when we move from private morality into the realm of borderline moral concerns and then fully professional domains for action.

In one's professional life, definitions of morality could well lead to the establishment of a very different set of prohibitions which would adhere more closely to legal and/or organizational protocols and limits than to moral codes of behavior. Public morality is defined more by your role or position in life and the expectations of behavior in those positions than to anything internal. Your obligations and responsibilities direct how you act, and oftentimes how you feel. Codes of professional ethics or behavior are intended to shape public morality; all professional degree programs require some form of ethics course/curriculum coverage. These codes tend to be a bit superficial and obvious, too easy to accommodate, too situational, and mostly address how we relate to the job. Professional ethics can be more easily clouded, or avoided, or minimized in the pursuit of acceptable job performance. Don't break the law. Don't cook the books. Don't discriminate or harass, etc. Rarely do such codes provide guidance in the difficult (and oftentimes ambiguous) situations managers confront where real ethical choices are required.

Then there are borderline private/professional values, such as the spectrum of lying in which there are "good" lies or acceptable lies and "bad" or unacceptable lies, or the "flexibility" one applies when managing the fiscal affairs of an organization. Everyone lies, at home and at work, but I believe we are able to distinguish amongst lies as to which are acceptable in what context. Everyone (I think) bends the rules a bit in the fiscal arena when strict regulations make it difficult to effectively manage.

I am simply asserting that it is hard to be two different people at the same time with two different codes of behavior, so every effort must be made to reconcile private and public morality. And when there is a divergence which you cannot overcome, where the conflict is simply too profound, at least understand the consequences when a choice is made. Or think about changing either your life or your work. There are way too many people who discover, at some point in their lives, that they cannot reconcile their dueling value structures, their dueling (or dual) visons of who they are and want to be.

Second, my upbringing has taught me, and I firmly believe, that the world was made broken and that it is my obligation and responsibility to play a role in fixing what is broken. This is the concept of "tikkun olam," a Hebrew phase commonly cited, even in non-sectarian settings. However humble and limited and perhaps misguided or arrogant that role may be, the choice to play the role is not mine. Deeply understood, there is in fact no choice to be made. It is one small connection, or obligation, to being a human living in a social context. "Fixing" may apply to an individual, a community, society .... or as a manager, the mission and work of an organization, the quality implementation of programs or advocacy for important policies. Irrespective of what job I've had or have, I must see it through this lens. Therefore, there is no immediate definitional concern, only an embedded code of behavior which everyone possesses in one form or another which would guide private action.

The presumption that there is a "good" core within each person is a belief closely held by many, but it is equally a belief challenged by much of what we see in the world of political discourse. As a former political philosophy major in college, I never quite got over the Hobbesian (Thomas Hobbs) view of humankind as "...nasty, brutish and short" (either in the state of nature or in reality), but I'm working on it, obligated to work on it. Possibly, applying the value of "tikkun olam" to public actions is one way of thinking about social justice. I use this expression to convey my message, but in every religion or every civil society, similar beliefs can be found.

Third, if I can revert to my old dissertation days when considering the design of public policies, we have an obligation to figure out in what circumstances we adhere to a particular philosophical construct when engaging in decision making and/or the implementation of any actions. Philosophy and management do in fact connect in real time! When I say this to students, they look at me with strange expressions on their faces. When I have suggested something like this to my peers, they are reaffirmed in their belief that I sometimes get stuck in another obtuse universe, forever tied to an academic mentality. Philosophical construct? Who, me? The answer is yes, every day, either implicitly or explicitly, though it would be nice if people accepted the reality and not simply the tacit acceptance of this human condition. There are many such philosophical constructs, built into our brains at some stage in our development, but to make my point I will suggest three.

For the most part, we survive as managers and leaders by adhering to a **utilitarian model which posits that for any particular policy, decision or action, there is a net gain (benefits less costs, including adverse impact on some people) to be had in whatever form of measurement we are applying.** We may be intending to do only good or correct things in our decision making, but believing that everyone gains with every one of our decisions is a bit naïve. This principle can apply to the allocation of organizational resources, e.g. space, money, influence; or the support of selected policies or strategies e.g. tax reform, placement of unwanted public facilities in local neighborhoods; or even the ways in which we nurture and recognize talent, e.g. granting of raises or promotions. This is not a zero-sum game, but simply postulates that if the majority benefit, or if the aggregate good is clear and quantifiable, then inevitably there are those on the "wrong" side of the aggregate. And yes, they might be angry or upset or claim a lack of fairness. Such is life. Utilitarianism is so built in to our decision-making processes that we are not even aware that this is a specific (but not the only) way of addressing the world. I can hardly think of times when I didn't act this way, and lived with both the positive and negative (both inevitable) consequences.

There are circumstances when a quite different approach can be used, one which posits that **no legitimate policy or decision should result in anyone being made worse off, though all may not benefit to the same extent.** There are no "losers" in this philosophical construct; there are, mostly, winners to varying degrees. There is, instead, a general sense of fairness which is recognized and accepted. This is not a matter of aggregation so much as a careful distribution or balancing of benefits. The examples of different decision situations referenced above could easily be reframed to fit this construct. The "open-space" office configuration is partly an attempt to equalize this resource (even if everyone is equally unhappy in not having private space). Instituting a "democratized" or participatory decision-making process instead of top-down management is another example. Giving everyone a raise (with a few getting a better "market-rate adjustment") is another strategy. Implementing new tax policy which benefits everyone (but to varying degrees) is perhaps more currently relevant. Thinking in this way is a clear departure from strict utilitarian thinking. We begin with a mindset and the mindset frames our actions. To be realistic, this approach has a great deal of appeal, but in many contexts, is not so easy to design or implement. There is no such thing as a free lunch. Costs and benefits are, in most contexts, hard or impossible to quantify.

The third construct is another example of applied philosophy, namely those who believe **their decisions, their professional judgments, can only legitimately be judged on a longitudinal time frame.** Utilitarian or fairness arguments are temporarily set aside or ignored because they cannot, as yet, be properly measured. The underlying principle is clear: "history will prove me right." This construct is, admittedly, my favorite since I've spent so many years as an organizational leader trying to convince myself and others that time would prove me to be right even if my immediate short-term decisions made a few folks worried or unhappy (or worse or better off). Time now becomes the critical dimension, the final arbiter, in determining what was a good or bad decision, a good or bad policy choice, success or failure. History becomes the judge, though what constitutes a clear time dimension to history is unclear. Recalling my comments on legacy and the importance of memory, if I'm wrong, in all likelihood I won't be around to suffer the negative consequences; and if I was right, someone else will probably reap the glory of positive consequences.

Fourth, and finally, in framing social justice as a central leadership issue, there is the choice or obligation to understand where you fall on the implicit behavioral scale provided by Machiavelli and others. If a choice is to be made, would you rather be "loved" or "feared" in the exercise of your role? Even if we loosely define what these terms mean (e.g. perhaps using terms like "respected" and "admired" would be better), and for the moment give Machiavelli the benefit of the doubt, the choice of managerial character and style is inevitable. Becoming comfortable with balancing the kind, caring, thoughtful parts of your leadership style with the potentially cruel, depersonalized, harsh implications of your actions is a daily demand of leadership.

Machiavelli, and others, may get bad press these days, but has anyone written a better management text book for those who must learn and know the costs and benefits associated with decisions which affect others? Has anyone better stated the benefits and costs of leadership? The endless list of managerial "how-to" books describing the huge variety of managerial styles, rarely confront real-time moral dilemmas. For me, there is no more realistic example of this dilemma than the times I have had to fire people for a variety of reasons, few of them tied to any specific negative cause. I knew I was hurting people, knew I was disrupting their lives, knew they could well hate me for years, and knew that in the short run I might well be hurting my own organization for some length of time. The same could be said about the many times I had to decide whether to continue an important and successful program which was losing its funding. In all cases, I believed I was acting in the best interests of the organizations I was leading. The stress felt by almost everyone in a managerial position oftentimes connects to this reality: we are expected to – frequently required to – accept this emotional burden.

On a personal level, one can be committed to fixing the world, living by a strict code of private moral rules, always being fair and just in making decisions, but sometimes act more or less harsh or severe in living and acting this way. I've given four suggestions for structuring how we deal with social justice, but how they fit together for any one person is a challenge. Avoiding the trap, or advantages, of situational ethics seems to be impossible. If we place all choices into the basket of situational ethics, we are nowhere.

Being at the Table and a Life of Value Compromise

As a manager, or leader, a critically important bottom line issue for me or anyone (and the organization one represents) is whether or not you are "at the table"! What table was that? Every table concerning social justice at which I could get a seat. The more tables, the better. The smaller the table, the more valuable the seat. The more important the domain of the table, the more vital it was to have a seat. Did it matter, ultimately, that being at any table may or may not have made the slightest difference or had any subsequent impact? Not really. Being at the table was (is) its own end, a necessary means to an end, irrespective of the substantive issues underlying the existence of the table. Everything I have said about social justice concentrates on this issue. Believing in social justice, fighting for social justice, advocating for social justice, possessing a philosophy predicated on a social justice theme, mean much more if you are at the table where social justice is the central (implicit or explicit) story line.

Being at the table implies the possession and use of power, influence, impact, status, a voice in vital social justice concerns. It demands an unavoidable willingness to negotiate, to deal, to win a few and maybe lose a few. There is no getting around this fact, this dilemma. Being dogmatic or virtuous or convinced that you are right are not effective strategies. You will not be listened to, you won't be invited back, you won't achieve your ends if you're not willing to play the game. You won't be a player. You will be relegated to the backbench. This is where conflicting philosophical constructs compete. This is where personal and professional values resolve their differences. This is when you go home and say, "what am I doing and who am I?"

And how do you get invited to have a seat? Many factors are important: the public standing of the organization you represent; your earned or acknowledged talent and reputation; your knowledge of issues being considered; your demographic profile; your list of friends and enemies; and, of course, good fortune and luck. But perhaps most important, from the vantage point of this essay, are the ways in which you are (known to be) willing to balance reputation and effectiveness and power with your social justice principles and goals and your organizational responsibilities. Ultimately, my definition of social justice when in a position of leadership is shaped by what you are willing to pay to achieve that which you believe.

I have not (or barely) mentioned any specific social justice issues. I have said nothing about believing in social equity, economic opportunity, quality programs for all populations, favorable immigration policies, higher minimum wage, environmental sanity, addressing global warming, access to affordable housing, freedom of the press, and on and on and on. My focus is on how you take these or other principles and fit them into a managerial philosophy, a model for leadership. But it would be foolish and disingenuous for me not to assert that the divisiveness concerning values and social justice and public policies has been damaging to our communities and our country. I can understand differences, even strong differences, on many public policy issues. I can't understand cruelty, mean-spiritedness, selfishness, self-aggrandizement at the expense of others.

Why Cannot We Agree on a Common Definition of Social Justice

Conversations about social justice should be straightforward and non-controversial since we all agree on what this term means in a civil society. But wait! Not really. We live in divisive times, when, since it connects to time, social justice means one thing in some of our urban centers, and quite another when you cross state or even city or town lines and blue fades to purple or red. Irrespective of colors, we now understand that we live where others like us live, read what others like us read, socialize with others who think like we do, watch TV or use social media that others like us utilize, find and stay with partners with whom we share political as well as social values. Facts and "alternative facts" seemingly have equal value in today's world. And yet, many of us live and go about our daily workplace lives by assuming a common understanding of what social justice means in America. This is a topic I would love to avoid, or confront head-on, or ignore, but cannot. By necessity, then, I will come at it from my own perspective. Envision two scenarios:

In situation one, the faculty, full and part-time, are sitting around the table, arguing about the concept of social justice, the "tag line" which defines this graduate program in non-profit management leadership and its companion social work program.

"We need to agree on a single definition which we can all espouse in class and which will guide all of our syllabi. This definition should be obvious and straightforward and incorporated in every syllabus."

"Why don't a few of us get together, draft a definition, and present it to everyone. Who wants to volunteer? Should we only have full time faculty in the group since they are the ones most committed to finding a definition and to the integrity of the school?"

"Don't you think there's a difference between how academicians and practitioners see this issue?"

"There is no one definition for social justice, especially when we consider professional practice. We all know it when we see it, especially if we agree to stay in New York City to teach and work."

"Aren't most of our jobs, for those of us in the field, defined by our belief in social justice? If this is the case, why do we need a single definition?"

"Isn't it better for the students if they understand we have varying perspectives on the concept, so they can figure out what social justice means for themselves?"

In the second situation, the selection committee for a newly created book award designed to recognize and honor contributions to the field of social justice, met to make a decision. The committee members (myself among them), came from diverse professional fields. Each person had to read twenty-eight books over a few months, submitted by the publishers and all released within a defined one year period. Neither the sponsors of the award, nor the publishers, provided any real definition of social justice except a very general statement on a few current social issues. The range of topics covered by the submittals was fascinating: deficiencies in the criminal justice system with strong racial implications; addressing the AIDS crisis; different interpretations of economic and social inequality; and several unique "inspirational" stories of personal redemption, or finding a meaningful advocacy role. The quality of the writing varied tremendously, and the editing was almost non-existent. Some submittals had no apparent connection to the social justice theme at all, and a few subjects were barely touched upon. The five jurors actually needed only an hour or so to pick the five semi-finalists, and then one winner from among that group. Somehow, in our roles as jurors, we "felt" what social justice meant. And we agreed that the "theme," though important, was so broad as to defy any common ground as to what constitutes social justice.

The above definitional debate continues at the university where I have taught for several years as an adjunct, meeting after meeting, semester after semester, with no resolution, no progress on consensus, no methodology for counting angels on the head of a pin. This debate, at least in my experience, is more likely to be held in an academic than a professional environment, if only because there is more time to engage in esoteric discussions when a decisive conclusion has no deadline and daily life is not affected. It could, however, just as easily be held at any gathering of non-profit leaders or government employees and elected officials, or in any forum where we argue amongst ourselves even when we have similar views or argue against others with dissimilar views. Even selecting a book award winner generates debate on meaning. Lack of consensus has not stopped us from having discussions about social justice in our communities, or in America overall.

Can there ever be a definitional resolution in such a divisive social and political environment as now characterizes our country? Is there a resolution which would bind the world of academic discourse with the world of professional practice? Do we even need such a resolution to guide our daily lives? Can we ever agree on how to label and address intractable problems with unproven or unworkable policies and actions? Aren't we mostly having these discussions or arguments with people just like us, where differences are subtle and rhetorical, rather than substantive? Are we ever in a situation where we are arguing with people not like us who have genuinely different views on the subject, either to convince them to think differently or simply to have a cathartic experience? And who has enough time to waste interacting with those having different views when real issues of social justice require our immediate attention and action? We act as leaders; therefore, we are expected to believe....in something.

As actors in the non-profit universe, these may well be unanswerable questions. Next to endless discussions about mission, talking about social justice is the next closest thing to feeling we have entered a conversational quagmire. Social justice may be the underlying premise of our incredibly diverse field, with a presumed tacit understanding of what social justice implies on a personal, professional and organizational level. But should we care about or allow this higher-order inquiry to interfere with how we perform? As managers and leaders, we act. We make decisions, manage organizations, implement and sometimes shape policies. Definitional uncertainty is a hassle, but not an insurmountable barrier. There are no syllabi to guide our practice, nor should there be. Tacit understanding of social justice may be sufficient.

I know I am not writing for everyone, and scholarly inquiry is well beyond my intellectual capacity or attention span. I am a practitioner, writing for other practitioners. If pressed, I can clearly espouse my views on many or all social justice issues, and be convinced (and even convincing) that I am correct in my thinking. More importantly, as I have said many times to my students in class, I don't necessarily care what anyone's explicit definition for social justice happens to be at this moment, or even what any individual's beliefs may be on specific issues. As an educator, I am more interested in how personal definitions and personal beliefs will affect and define someone as a manager and leader. For my former employees and those friends whom I still advise, my guidance is the same. I am interested in their espoused personal value structures and their understanding of social justice up to a point, but the bottom line is that I must focus primarily on how well they are doing their work, how values are converted into actions, or how I can best advise them on their jobs.

My primary concern is how you translate your personal and professional beliefs (and social justice definitions) into the daily obligations and responsibilities of leadership. How is your judgment – evident to yourself and to the world – affected by questions which are almost impossible to resolve or reconcile? Social justice may be a bit abstract, but good management and leadership is anything but abstract. I have to believe, or hope, that managers and leaders do in fact have values which drive their actions.

This essay has studiously avoided views on specific social justice issues, e.g. immigration policies or sexual harassment or economic equity. I take this position because others have pontificated about their views on every possible topic which falls under the social justice tent. I'm not sure what I can add to this discourse, and I'm guessing that my personal views would be obvious to anyone reading between the lines. Instead, I have offered advice or direction on the concept of **framing social justice as a way of organizing one's approach to management and leadership** while trying to avoid any distracting ideological or value positions on myriad social justice arguments. I have to trust that my ideology and values are transparent if not openly stated. Social justice is, for me, an **internally driven concept**, eventually manifested in visible application and explicit definitional meaning.

Essay Four

Risk and Possible Failure as
Key Ingredients for Success

At a recent panel I attended, designed as a debate between two highly respected veterans from the philanthropic community, the central question being asked was the extent to which effective philanthropy was dependent on high quality performance outcome measures achieved by the grantees. Could there be (either) one without the other, and if one was to prevail which would it be? The question was rhetorical, meant to spur an entertaining fight among friends, but most of the folks in the audience knew there was no correct answer. The human services sector these days, as with other sectors of our economy, is driven by outcome measures, so to that extent philanthropy could not separate itself from common practice and the demands of evaluation. Effective philanthropy? This seems to depend on who the philanthropist happens to be and/or what the foundation/trust/individual uses as guiding principles in distributing resources. Grappling with the multi-dimensions of why people/institutions give money away is seen by many as beyond rational discourse.

As a member of the audience, I used this forum to ask one of my favorite unresolved questions of the donor-set. How do you acknowledge and reward risk-laden organizational or personal behavior which is conducted in the pursuit of important organizational goals? When I've had the opportunity, this single question has blossomed into related questions. How do you reward and acknowledge bold strategic moves or initiatives which could expand the current organizational mission? How do you ensure that occasional failure or minimal success in these pursuits does not immediately result in the punishment of those who try when the attempts are sound and defensible? Shouldn't risk taking within an enlightened management framework be encouraged?

These questions could and should be directed as well to the different levels of government which fund the programs operated by non-profits. The symbiotic relationship which exists between the public and nonprofit sectors has been integral to the provision of a comprehensive array of services for generations, but these relationships have evolved over time. It is safe to say that allowances for risk, for experimental programming, for testing hypotheses, even for encouraging entrepreneurial ventures in the non-profit community, are rarely granted by our public funding sources.

Relationships among risk, failure and reward exist in all sectors, but the ground-rules differ tremendously. This essay focuses on the non-profit and public sectors, so commenting on how the private sector deals with risk and innovation is beyond my scope. Presumably, in the private sector, the "market" incorporates and accounts for almost predictable proportions of successes and failures in almost all domains. There is no universal expectation of inevitable success. Brands fail, campaigns fail, retail shops fail, restaurants fail, tech devices fail, stocks fall, and so on. No big deal. Failure is built into the cost models associated with any and all specific parts of the economy. People lose money, jobs, status, all as routine costs of doing business. But the market economy is built on growth and success. Brands succeed, campaigns succeed, shops succeed, restaurants succeed, tech devices succeed, the market goes up. People are rewarded on some measurable scale both for trying and for succeeding.

In the public sector, some programs or policies last forever, some age out, and a few are tried and occasionally fail, though the term "fail" is rarely used. The "aging out" or slow disappearance or renaming of programs (same money, new labels) may better describe how things happen. It's more like, well, we tried and it didn't quite work so we'll try something different. Rarely are people negatively affected by failure within the government sector, nor are they especially rewarded. Sustained employment is frequently the best currency. Memory is in short supply. Risky behavior and exciting innovation occur only rarely, usually associated with the recognition of new crises or challenges or the whims of an elected official. This excitement lasts only for a while.

For some reason, we tend to look at the non-profit sector differently, where cost/business models and value propositions do not allow for or easily accommodate either risk, failure, or innovation. I don't mean this as a global proposition, but more as the norm. To challenge this norm, I would offer a few counter-arguments, a few propositions which could alter the playing field.

Non-profits, in their contractual relationships with the government sector, must be allowed to operate with a few of the most basic elements of a market-based system. Actions related to this proposition have been put forth for decades, with minimal progress. The actions relate to the most basic rules of competition and market based behavior: (a) initial price determination for "goods or services" provided by the non-profits to the public should be subject to fair negotiation and determination of "value" and appropriate "outcomes" (rather than government determination of allowable price irrespective of costs); (b) incentives for enhanced quality and quantity of "outcomes" should be built into the pricing structure (instead of penalties for not achieving contractual obligations which may not be mutually determined and reasonable in the first place); (c) understanding that "profit" and "surplus" mean the same thing in many ways and should be equally recognized and incorporated in any contract. Each of these is more complicated than I have defined, but they share a common element: they are not being practiced today. The last point, that profit and surplus have much in common, may be the most controversial.

Some would argue that non-profits, by definition, cannot make a profit, and therefore have no access to revenue which is used for various purposes in the for-profit world. On a practical level, this is not accurate. Non-profits can generate surpluses, i.e. excess of revenues over expenses, if their contracts cover full operational costs and if they have other sources of revenue. Surpluses can be used for, among other things, salary increases or increases in benefit packages or bonuses; equipment purchase or capital improvements; costs associated with acquisition of other non-profits; marketing and development expenses; increases in reserves, etc. Surpluses cannot be used to distribute to owners (there are none!), or for unreasonable compensation (actually not regulated very closely). The boundaries between sectors should be and are increasingly more blurred, as well they should be.

More venture capital funds can and should be put into the sector by either the private sector, the philanthropic community, or government agencies, to allow for qualitative and quantitative improvements and expansion. The non-profit sector, with few individual exceptions, is substantially under-capitalized, hindering its ability to produce the quality and quantity of programs which are needed and expected. Very few non-profits have either their own capital or access to capital to engage in entrepreneurial activities which may lead to innovation, replication, and other measures of success. When endowments or Board-reserved funds exist at whatever scale, and are properly managed, the principal is expected to be preserved for longer-term stability and only the income or part of the increased value are available for immediate use. The sector has grown used to this weakness, focusing instead on smaller incremental suggestions for longer-term survival and sustainability. There is a need to think bigger. There is a need for a non-profit version of an IPO!

There should be a return to the world of pilot and demonstration projects, with different approaches funded at the same time and organizations compensated for their efforts. In the good-old-days, foundations funded pilot or demonstration projects which were intended to test or prove the value of new programs or initiatives. Those that succeeded were then expected to be supported on a longer-term basis by new government support or even greater private support. Programs which were less successful, or just plain failed, were studied as to the reasons. These days, there are few if any such enterprises. Most private funders want some assurance of success; foundations tend to be, irrespective of what they preach, risk averse. Government will fund new programs, especially in emerging areas of interest, but as noted they are set up under non-market constraints and to minimize risk.

Finally, we must overcome the stereotypical and mutually reinforcing perspectives that non-profit leaders feel government is ineffective, uncreative and slow while government officials/ employees feel non-profits are trying to rip off public money and care more about their survival than about the programs they offer and the people they serve. These attitudes might not be explicitly expressed on a regular basis, but the systemic relationships set up between these worlds reinforce the point I am making.

Failure or limited success is NOT synonymous with or even to be associated with issues of incompetence, wrong-thinking, lack of strategic planning, poor judgment, or the impact of unanticipated negative events. I am interested in that class of actions/decisions/ policies where the objectives and goals have been well thought out and should be pursued even if pursuit involves uncertainties, unexplored paths, potential points of conflict, and disappointment with results.

Essay Five

Issues Concerning Risk, or the Subject Frequently Discussed and Rarely Actualized

The original version of this essay appeared in 2015, was revised several times, and appeared as one of the Appendices in the report prepared by the Human Services Council of New York, entitled New York Nonprofits in the Aftermath of FEGS: A Call to Action (2015). I was a member of the Commission which produced that report, and one of the strong advocates for emphasizing the importance of **risk assessment and management** in strengthening the sector. Several excellent studies prepared by SeaChange Capital Partners in association with Oliver Wyman provided much needed substantive research supporting the need for in-depth assessment, with the first report focusing on New York and a second larger study addressing national issues. Several for-profit and non-profit organizations have since developed important new tools enabling non-profits to engage in comprehensive self-generated risk analysis, with follow-up technical assistance made available including Community Resource Exchange, (CRE). In 2017, I did a podcast on the subject of risk (see Risk Alternatives' Podcast Episode 20:

Learning Risk Management from a Nonprofit Veteran: A Podcast Interview with Michael Zisser).

This essay is a greatly expanded version of my original effort at discussing this subject from a practicing professional's managerial perspective. The field of risk assessment has grown considerably in recent years with many more consultants and technical assistant providers filling a much-needed gap in available resource expertise. As with the other essays in this collection, my intention is to offer simple direct advice on this important subject. I am neither competing with nor serving as a substitute for the other expertise/ tools you will need to conduct a comprehensive risk assessment and management strategy.

I will focus, therefore, on briefly outlining **ten** key risk assessment issues, each of which requires more discussion and analysis than this essay can cover. This is a checklist of issues to think about, with specific advice offered, not to be missed or minimized in your managerial work-load.

(1) Taking programmatic risks is what the non-profit world is all about. Successfully managing risk is what defines strong governance, leadership, and management. We must begin with this basic premise when considering risk. Too often, an organization's introduction to risk analysis is seen as dealing with or discovering negative issues, weaknesses, or potential crises. This storyline must be reversed. There is nothing worse in our world than a risk averse organization, or risk averse staff or risk averse Board leadership. There is nothing better than an organization or leadership reasonably well prepared to prepare for and manage risk when it occurs in the pursuit of an organization's mission.

Denial of the possibility or existence of risk is pervasive, and at some point, not resolvable. Leaders are not praised or rewarded for taking on or resolving risk situations (unless they're in the private sector). And yet the history of the non-profit sector, and the sector's obligations in the future, relate directly to addressing key social issues with programs or entrepreneurial ventures which are intended to succeed but may possibly fail. Failures are not always documented, but many important innovations have occurred within the context of experimentation (e.g. conducting pilot programs which are evaluated and then either halted or put into general practice). We must begin on an affirmative note for a mistakenly labeled negative phenomenon. The central point of organizational strategic planning is developing the capacity to mitigate whatever risk might occur, and knowing what level of risk is tolerable.

(2) Very few managers of non-profit human service organizations have studied the concept of risk in any professional or educational context, so this subject has remained primarily "self-taught." Very few graduate programs or advanced management certificate programs offer in-depth courses on the subject. These issues could be taught (to some extent), in educational settings or on the job or in some other forums, but it is not in our culture to always be asking of ourselves and our organizations, "what are all the things which could go wrong in any given decision or situation," or "how do I build an organization which can withstand and address any potential risk situation." One can always get consultant or technical assistance advice to address risk issues, but my first piece of advice is this. **You need to be self-aware enough to recognize that risk is ever present; you may need help coming from any number of directions; you cannot afford to be sanguine about obvious evidence; understand that surprises are inevitable;**

realize that success and failure are two sides of the same coin; relish the fact that risk is endemic to our purpose. Paying for assistance is the second step, not the first.

There are many managers who grow up to be excellent at assessing and managing risk, though I can't describe the path to such competency other than experience and utilizing applied judgment. Clearly, most non-profits survive the endless list of challenges which come along. But more and more nonprofits either are failing or are close to failure, vulnerable on fronts known and unknown, coping with sustainability questions and/or paths to further success. Managing risk is about self-awareness, self-confidence, strong leadership, irrespective of the specific substantive area of risk we may be considering.

(3) Financial risk analysis is the most commonly understood, the most observable, and to a large extent the most manageable risk factor. This is also the domain where inside and outside support and advice is most readily available, so all I will do is list the many functional areas covered under this risk factor with the most elemental management advice.

Financial risk could cover some or all of the following topics.

(a) **The financial and program implications of performance based contracting are by definition high risk ventures where the full value of a contract can be achieved only if certain (sometimes unattainable) conditions are met. Never agree to a contract where an organization is obligated to budget or expense 100% of the contract irrespective of goal attainability.** It is much safer to budget for spending closer to 90% of the contract (as a suggested %), allowing for some flexibility and possibly allowing for an operational "surplus" if all measures are met. Note that performance-based contracts are rarely if ever designed to allow for a "profit" or surplus if the outcome measures exceed the contractual goals.

(b) Lease obligations as a longitudinal risk carry no operational or audit requirement other than stating the aggregate liability over time. There is no operational or audit obligation to document off-setting income sources to cover the lease obligation. Few if any government program contracts extend for the general length of time required by most lease agreements. **Never sign a lease agreement unless you have the right "escape clauses" which enable you to withdraw from the agreement if specified funding sources covering the lease are lost or expired.** The only exception to this managerial rule would be if the organization happens to have a high demand for additional (funded) space and is experiencing over-crowding of other existing space.

This type of lease agreement is more common than one would imagine, especially in areas were the landlord could readily re-lease the space and/or in areas where any reasonably stable tenant is better than carrying empty space. But there is no question that one of the biggest growing organizational liabilities is unfilled space, which if not covered by contract funds must be paid for by general operational funds. The bottom line for any organization? Better to be crowded in affordable space than to take on risky longitudinal obligations.

The possibility of having a very long-term lease agreement (e.g. with government owned properties or through a ground lease) may be the way to go when and if possible, especially if capital investment in improving the property is necessary. But even in this context, escape clauses should be considered, or the risk of larger organizational failure factored in as a risk variable.

The possibility of **acquiring** additional space is more complicated than I can address here. Owning space is an asset; leases are liabilities. Owning heavily leveraged space drifts towards the liability category. Owning space outright (with minimal debt obligations) is a longer-term protection against financial failure. Owning space means you're responsible for keeping it up (and paying attention to depreciation schedules!). Leasing space means you can deflect some of the major maintenance obligations, and rely on the landlords to keep the facility in good repair. As noted before, very few leaders in the non-profit sector have "real estate" experience or know-how to make the correct short or long-term space decisions. This expertise can be added to the Board, or acquired elsewhere.

(c) **The potential for Medicaid or other third-party payments or reimbursements at less than 100% of submittals for various legitimate or other reasons is inevitable.** There are always outright disallowances for payments, or incorrect requests for payment, which make the 100% reimbursement completely unrealistic. Even the best and most diligent Medicaid billing staff and fiscal oversight within an organization cannot overcome this reality. More diligent "Medicaid fraud" oversight by government actors broadly interprets the concepts of fraud or over-payment which results in very strict interpretation of allowable Medicaid reimbursements. The managerial response to this important issue is simple. **Allow for a reasonable and historically accurate rate of reimbursement, based on prior years of billing (better to budget at the 85-90% rate). Most importantly, create a FUNDED Medicaid liability on your books to cover any reclaiming of funds by the government.** The worst that can happen by under-estimating the rate of return is that you beat the rate and get more revenue than expected. As obvious as this may sound, the number of non-profits which carry no or minimal liability and which run into trouble is scary. This has led to bankruptcy or the obligation to pay back the government over time through deductions from future Medicaid reimbursements.

(d) **Set up in the fiscal record keeping system (and in cash as much as possible!!) a set of "funded" liabilities** (in addition to Medicaid) **to cover likely or projected losses or obligations, including but not limited to: accrued vacation, possible anticipated or unanticipated layoff or severance packages, retirement packages for senior executives, and depreciation.** Again, unfunded liabilities have become one of the leading factors in nonprofits being subject to potential bankruptcy or disruption if even modest things go wrong. Government contracts rarely if ever cover these liabilities. Union agreements and/or personnel practices obligate the organization to cover these liabilities. The "assets and liabilities" of an organization are evident in an audit, but are neither required nor incorporated in an annual budget – unless funded!

(e) **Facility or maintenance emergency issues, or possibly known significant facility expenses not covered by current income, are inevitable and uncontrollable and unpredictable. The risk of disrupted occupancy, for whatever reason, may be covered by insurance (business disruption). Having a building reserve fund is the best option for facility expenses.** An appropriate line of credit also helps. Well connected organizations may have the option of pressuring government funding sources to cover facility emergencies if loss of the program is at stake.

(4) **Non-profit organizations agree to sign government contracts and provide services irrespective of the potential risks of implementing the contracts because:** they feel they must do so, are tempted to operate the programs, want to grow in scale, believe the contractual programs are mission related, don't care if they are or are not mission related, are pressed by Boards or organizational leaders or some other interested stakeholders to do the work, or fear for their survival and future standing in a competitive environment. **This ubiquitous process of agreeing to conduct high-risk programs must stop, or be rigidly managed by the application of criteria which would help guide an organization in agreeing to conduct programs which are sustainable and which minimize short and long-term risk.** Careful analysis of the rationale for signing contracts is rare. Most contracts are non-negotiable with the government ("sign or don't do the work") and many lawyers would probably advise nonprofits against signing any government contract given the terms of the agreements - except that we have no choice. NO contract a non-profit has with any government agency is negotiated or created between equals players, though this unbalanced approach may be slowly changing in some situations. Very few are designed to

be "fully loaded" as to ascertaining the true cost of providing the contracted services. Such is the reality of our sector. Tools have been developed by our sector to examine and rate the viability of government contracts (e.g. the tools developed by the Human Services Council of New York) and the risks involved in signing any agreement, but these tools do not necessarily address the reasons why we sign or choose not to sign.

(5) **It must be clear who within an organization needs to understand risk analysis in its broadest or most specific dimensions. It should be painfully obvious that every possible interpretation of risk be on someone's agenda and within his/ her area of responsibility and expertise since no one person can be responsible for all factors.** Since every issue eventually rises to the top - for the staff as well as the Board - the CEO and Board Chair must know about the dimensions but not necessarily be expert in all areas. The following questions must be asked and clearly answered: (a) which staff is knowledgeable of and responsible for each risk factor; **(b) has an organizational "culture" of risk assessment been built in and is it operational and transparent;** (c) is the Board fully informed and knowledgeable about risk factors; (d) does the Board have one or more people specifically assigned to risk analysis. If the organization utilizes one of the risk assessment tools now available, will the staff and Board responsible for answering the questions know how to answer and be fully honest?

There are NO direct questions regarding risk which are explicitly asked in ANY of the legal documents which non-profits are obligated to complete (e.g. annual audits, 990s, A-133 reviews, etc.). A careful integrated analysis of ALL these documents may provide a better understanding of risk factors. Nor are risk factors a primary subject in most strategic plans. Understanding risk factors is not the same as charting the strengths and weaknesses of an organization.

(6) **There is no real way to protect against internal fraud other than strict internal controls – and relying on extraordinary levels of trust.** Any good auditor should be providing or advising on all of the steps to ensure fraud can be detected and addressed (actually a requirement). However, a reasonably skilled – though nefarious – fiscal person could probably pull off a fraudulent scheme. Most get caught. Some don't get caught until too late. **Make sure you have sufficient fraud insurance, which has several sub-categories. Make sure your bank relationships are solid and protect you against any form of bank fraud** (e.g. trying to cash fake checks or payroll is ubiquitous these days and should be caught and covered by the banks). Many non-profits are probably either under-insured or are missing certain types of coverage, an easily fixable and only marginally expensive issue. Finally, pay whatever it takes to hire a fully trustworthy Chief Financial Officer. They are harder to find than a Chief Executive Officer.

(7) **There is NO way to protect an organization from the risk of incompetent, dangerous, dishonest, or even nice people who can hurt the organization in ways hard to imagine. Unfortunately, it is too often part of our culture to be hesitant in removing, criticizing or correcting such people. Advice in addressing this all-to-common phenomenon is easy: have access to a very good (hopefully pro bono) lawyer skilled in personnel practices; have the right insurance; pull the trigger fast on getting rid of such people; have a "liability" reserve fund to pay off bad actors as fast as possible.**

**(8) Reputational risk is, for most of us, the scariest issue
and one of the hardest to protect against.** A good reputation
can take years to build and seconds to lose. There are several
primary ways in which reputation can be impugned. These days,
the most common means is through the use of social media, when
a disgruntled employee, legitimately or not, attacks some or all of
the organization or particular members of the organization. Social
media attacks cannot be prevented or defended against. They are
to be tolerated, with strict discipline, and trust that time will take
care of the issue. Threatening to fight back, or actually fighting
back, rarely if ever helps. Whistle-blowers are a different story,
carry more legitimacy, and frequently are correct in their actions.
Part of the audit function is to actually set up the process by
which staff can inform a third party of perceived irregularities in
the organization. If there is legitimacy, then we jump to the issue
of adequate defense and insurance. The third major vulnerability
involves the multitude of formal audits and performance reviews
which can question and document organizational deficiencies.
From an audit perspective, being a "high risk" auditee for any
length of time is problematic and a public display of weakness.
In New York City, there is a structured review process known
as "Vendex" which, on a regular basis, assesses organizational
performance on several levels. A bad Vendex review (presumably
an accurate one) sits on your record forever, and can affect receiving
future contracts.

**Addressing reputational risk involves several technical and
personal managerial responses. On the technical side, never
lose sight of strict financial accountability. Never forget that
auditors are accountable to the Board, and not the staff. Never
forget that if you accept government funding you must know
how to play by the rules and regulations which come with**

the money. Remember that responding to reputational criticisms is as much a marketing as a substantive issue. Understand your insurance requirements (which some leaders consider to be a boring subject UNTIL they're not so boring).

On the personal side – and this is much more difficult – **show leadership patience if and when attacked, whether the attack is legitimate or not. Show confidence in your organization and your staff and your mission.** Quickly develop a strategy for rebuilding organizational confidence. And know when to move aside if necessary.

(9) **Little or no venture capital funding is available in our sector to take even modest risks or to cover against the downside of taking risks.** The few exceptions are small scale or too expensive to access. We have few non-profit versions of private equity firms or investment banks to support us. Most non-profits are severely under-capitalized, which means that taking risks is more risk-laden than should be the case, even if necessary. For organizations which either have capital or access to capital, establishing a "venture capital" fund should be considered, essentially removed from the obligation of providing a certain rate of short-term return on assets. **The only real answers are obvious and probably unattainable: (a) having Boards of Directors capable of creating such funds to protect the long-term sustainability of organizations; (b) convincing the private sector to invest in such funds as a form of social enterprise, either through grants or low-cost loans; (c) convincing government funding sources that capital investments in the non-profit sector are critically important to the survival and success of the sector. The upside of taking risks, which should be one of the basic principles of the sector, is that the returns will be substantial and beneficial.**

(10) Endowments or reserve funds, where they exist, are primarily targeted to supporting ongoing operations as common practice. This is, in itself, a risky concept and not supportive of an entrepreneurial enterprise. **A strategy gaining more widespread acceptance is that only a portion of an endowment's or reserve fund's return should be targeted to supporting ongoing operations while some of the return is set aside as potential "venture capital" reserves. This strategy potentially covers for the risk-seeking behavior in a healthy organization, protecting current operations while allowing for other important ventures.**

Essay Six

Thinking About Land Use Ventures for Non-Profits

People have asked, "how do you do an air rights deal, a zoning lot merger, a joint development project, a major renovation or a corporate acquisition involving real estate or land use?" As if I could or would answer these inquiries in a succinct phone conversation or over a single cup of coffee. Even if I could, why would I make the answer seem any less complex than it is in real life?

Our sector is increasingly confronted by these exciting possibilities, but is not necessarily prepared to successfully move forward. New skill sets, new sensibilities, new relationships, new understanding of revenue and expenses, are required. Doing "deals" is frequently only minimally about programs, with which we generally feel more comfortable, and a lot more about other factors and strategies.

There is a dearth of helpful stories or professional guides to provide a comprehensive path to assist non-profits in this ever-expanding arena. For example, there is no readily accessible "Land Use

Planning 101" manual for the sector. Quality organizations to support these ventures are rare, unlike in the private sector, and in high demand. Not all organizations have access to the necessary supports, pro bono or otherwise.

I've drafted a summary of "Strategic Issues" and "Selected Best Practices" just to set a foundation for those managers/leaders thinking about or initiating strategic deals. These notes might be helpful more to those in the human services sector; for those in the housing sector, these notes are more obvious. They are certainly not in any way exhaustive.

Before considering the following lists, remember a few key factors: (1) Understand your shorter and longer term organizational needs for space, money, expansion, and growth. This analysis should precede major real estate or land use moves, rather than the other way around. (2) Understand your current and future property needs and available resources. (3) Understand your personal interest in making the necessary investment in these processes, since commitment is an important variable.

Finally, I offer NO specifics regarding the details of any land use project or decision. For example, calculating what air rights you have and what they are worth and what City policies (or zoning regulations) may affect this information is beyond the present scope. Similarly, making a decision to acquire a property, sign a major lease expansion, or partner with a for-profit developer is serious business, with no appropriate short answer. These issues focus, instead, on how to think about moving forward, the first steps in what will always be a long-term process.

Strategic Issues

(1) Build the right planning and implementation team!

Any reasonably complicated real estate or land use project/ decision requires a set of experts representing skill sets well beyond the internal management and Board capacities of the typical organization. These experts would include but are not limited to: a law firm with expertise in either real estate or land use issues, which are not necessarily the same skill sets; a zoning analysis expert who may be present at a law firm but in all likelihood you will need a specialist in this area; an appraiser with experience in the type of project being considered; a law firm with expertise in cooperatives and condominiums (if appropriate to the project); architects capable of providing assistance and expertise at all stages of the project, from concept to preliminary schemes to final documents to development (if it gets that far) and who have access to the necessary engineers and other technical professionals; construction management support and expertise, preferably as an owner's representative. This would be considered the "external" team supporting top management and the Board.

(2) Make sure there is a team leader!

In building the team, and in ensuring that the team moves forward in a fully integrated manner, there must be a lead person in the organization with longitudinal investment in the organization and project. This person needs to know enough about each of the components of the project, enough about the contributions of each area of expertise, enough about the points raised below, to see the project through from beginning to end. Technical expertise in these areas is not a prerequisite! This could be the CEO, another top management person of the organization (thought this does not happen very often given the training of most CEOs), a designated knowledgeable Board member, or the owner's representative (an outside professional and member of the team). To repeat and emphasize, the leader should be committed to staying through the full length of project conception to completion, which could be years. The leader provides, at the very least, the VISION behind the venture.

(3) **The team may not be needed or operational all at once, but must be available on demand.**

The best news for an organization would be that all of this expertise was available whenever needed and pro bono, either coming from the Board, friends or other contacts. The upside of pro bono support is the cost! The possible down side is availability of the expertise and where you sit on their work priority list. Pro bono or paid for, the expertise must be highly qualified. You get what you "pay for" (which means that pro bono support is not helpful if not high quality). Almost any land use or real estate transaction can be very expensive to accomplish, which must be taken in to account with the project financing.

And since many projects never actually get implemented, it is important to avoid costs which cannot be made up if the project fails or is stopped for good reason. Members of the team must also be able and willing to stay engaged over an extended time frame, ready to work when the work is needed, since No project is ever completed on a predetermined schedule. Changing members of a team, like changing high level management staff, has considerable costs.

(4) **Think about the initial project numbers/budget, several times.**

Then think again about the interim numbers, several times. Then run the numbers again because they are never right and are dependent on many factors beyond your control. The numbers are constantly changing. And build in a HUGE error factor since no real estate or land use venture ever costs what people think it will cost. In the non-profit sector, margins of error are rarely considered let alone financed. Cost overruns are inevitable.

(5) Understand the longitudinal time dimension of real estate and land use decisions.

This is perhaps the hardest thing for non-profit management and Boards to fully understand and internalize. CEOs and their financial staffs in the housing field know this inherently as a way of life. Others in our sector usually work on a different clock, more attuned to program contracts and budgets. There is no such thing as an "annual" land use or real estate venture. A longer time dimension also means that risks are hard to enumerate ahead of time and almost impossible to avoid. Be prepared that the long-term benefits of the venture may exceed your tenure but be part of your legacy.

(6) Never forget or underestimate the role of financing, review and regulatory agencies involved with your project.

The list of external parties and stakeholders is based on the project, but it will be long and NOT under your control. These external parties are what make the longitudinal time frame so exasperating. There seems to be little/no interest at the various government levels to assist in expediting projects despite the rhetoric, so patience (and money for expert help) are essential.

(7) Keep the Board and other key stakeholders engaged!

Never get too far ahead of them or yourself. There will be too many points where the project could fall apart, where the direction and expectations will need to be reset and/or where more funds and support are needed. To minimize risk to you and the organization, be transparent and inclusive.

(8) **Trust no one.**

Don't trust time estimates, prices, construction estimates, expert advice, or anything else, but don't project that distrust! Build in multiple layers of risk analysis and tolerance, go with your instincts and your judgment. And try not to be too far wrong.

Selected Additional Best Practices

(1) Do not sign any leases without at least three conditions: (a) the right to terminate the lease at key stages if the funding sources which initially paid for the lease are lost and no suitable replacements are found; (2) the length of the lease should closely correspond to the funded length of the program contracts or grants which will occupy the space; (3) if space is used for administrative spaces, ensure that sufficient indirect or general support funds are available over the length of the contract to meet the obligation. All of these conditions are based on the unfortunate historical fact that too many non-profits over-extend themselves with leases which become liabilities well beyond anticipated revenue to cover them.

(2) The annual audit, usually in the Notes section, documents future-year lease obligations, which are above and beyond the liabilities contained in the current audit year. Have available for Board review the projected income sources to cover those

leases. The audit does not deal with future issues (except for certain debt obligations), but the Board/management review should consider projected revenue to cover longer term obligations.

(3) Have a reliable mechanism for keeping up with any violations or penalties associated with your properties, including those assessed by regulatory and oversight agencies (perhaps best done by hiring a service to do this for you), and make sure penalty payments are made on a timely basis.

(4) Avoid mortgages to the greatest extent possible, irrespective of the funder or terms! Owning property is always a temptation, but obviously requires a long-term commitment and presumption of off-setting income. Program contracts/grants rarely if ever match up with mortgage timelines. And we rarely "fund" a depreciation schedule so that resources are available for inevitable repairs or improvements. Our sector is "trained" to assume that such obligations will always be met one way or another, but this has proven not to be the case in an increasing number of circumstances.

(5) The pot of gold at the end of the real estate transaction (e.g. air rights sales, so-called "free" space in a private development, etc.) is not always what it seems (see item #4 above). Initial numbers can be enticing, but sometimes do not take into account replacement costs, time lost in transition, future operating expenses, living off-sight during the project implementation, a poor rate of return on investments, and so on. And when/if the money arrives in your account, you may feel better but it might not dramatically change your organizational life style.

For example, converting "air rights" into cash is converting one asset for another, and spending down assets is NOT what non-profits should be doing. There is a difference between having financial security and having disposable money to spend.

Complexity and risk are the key characteristics of any land use planning or real estate transaction, but these deals could be the best strategic decisions for your organization to consider. Bottom line, get the right assistance when and where you need it, and make sure the top management team and the Board are ready for an extended but hopefully productive journey.

Essay Seven

The Importance of (Occasionally) Questioning Political Correctness

Leaders and managers confront unpredictable issues on a daily basis, with few guidebooks to help them out. Experience should affirmatively influence how these issues are addressed, but not always. And experiences are frequently clouded or distorted by the rules of political correctness. Avoiding personal and organizational risk frequently prevents people from saying what sometimes needs to be said. Speaking "truth to power" is easy to say, but difficult to do – and what is truth anyway. **My general advice is: break free of political correctness in those moments when your organization, and your professional judgment demand this of you.**

Giving Credit to Others

I recently purchased a book on the increasingly popular topic of understanding and addressing risk in the non-profit sector. The content was of interest to me, but I was also curious as to who else was given credit by the authors – one of whom I have known for years - for doing similar or related work in this field since there have been relatively few engaged players. The short answer was virtually no one was given any credit for helping to shape the subjects addressed in the book. I don't believe this was a deliberate omission, and don't believe any slight was intended. Unfortunately, the norm in our field is to not think about giving credit to others as an earlier essay suggested, there is little recognition of history or context.

As a technical manual, a "how-to" exercise, the book was very informative and well presented, though it may have missed a few of the basic "reality" propositions that come with the subject (e.g. the limits of rationality, the cost of comprehensive strategizing). But the book isn't the issue and this is not intended as a review. **Giving credit to others is the issue.** In the academic community, scholars understand that being cited in other peoples' work is a sign of respect and accomplishment. Citing other people in the text or footnotes is a sign of professional acknowledgement for one's peers and recognition that no one is alone. In the non-profit community or in government sectors, there exists what can only be described as a deliberate disposition against respecting or acknowledging others' contributions, past or present.

I dare not venture as to the motivations for this phenomenon, which may be entirely idiosyncratic, though we can all guess. **Not giving credit is a sign of hubris, of arrogance, and is essentially unprofessional. And people do not forget when this happens. Giving credit is a sign of confidence, professionalism, and admiration for others' efforts.**

Sitting here in New York City, I can think of obvious examples. Universal PreK (Kindergarten) is considered a major social policy accomplishment by the current administration. The success of the UPK program is well deserved, but it is as much a "marketing" or "public relations" success as a programmatic innovation. In New York City and elsewhere, excellent public and private programs for 2-4 year olds (including Head Start) have existed for years if not generations. In effect, they have been cannibalized in the promotion and implementation of a "new program." New Mayor, new program name, with more funding and a few programmatic enhancements. But was any credit given to the predecessor programs which formed the conceptual and practical components for establishing UPK? No way.

The concept of locating jails and prisons (or half-way facilities or group homes) closer to the communities and families from which the facility "occupants" come is as old as the hills. Again in New York City, an amazingly innovative plan is now underway to close Rikers Island, literally an island in the East River which housed almost 9,000 people at the close of 2017. This may well be an excellent idea, but it is also almost exactly the same idea as presented several decades ago by another administration.

The former plan was never implemented, for reasons which will inevitably come into play again this time around. But the interesting point is that, as far as I can tell, not a single comment has been made by any of the current participants pushing this strategy that a prior plan existed. Moreover, the lessons learned the last time around may affect the outcome this time as well. **Understanding how others have dealt with complex problems is a vital leadership quality. Avoiding understanding is a recipe to repeat the failures of history and to possibly undermine current successes.** But was any credit given to the predecessor program? No way.

Addressing the homeless issue? Placing shelters in local communities? Using the market place to create subsidized housing as a small percentage of the units developed? Targeting public resources to specific neighborhoods with the premise that concentration will produce better results? Espousing fairness in addressing the "not in my backyard" issue (NIMBY) when the reality is always otherwise? Try and try again, hoping this time the plan will work better than the last time. Is trying again important? The answer is obviously YES. But was any credit given to those who have tried these methods in the past and sometimes succeeded and sometimes failed? No way. Examples abound in every community.

Board Diversity

The argument for governance and managerial diversity, in most contexts, has become a subject that does not appear to allow for dissenting viewpoints. By definition, Boards of nonprofits should be filled with representatives of the communities being served or which should be served. Sufficient representation, or governance control, by key stakeholders is now accepted as a self-evident end in itself. If this end cannot be immediately achieved, there should be a clear path to success with quantifiable progress being made. Is it safe to argue otherwise in a public forum? Clarity on representation is sometimes confusing, but not intended to diminish the value of the end goal. Does it apply to race, religion, sexual orientation, or any other category protected by fairly ubiquitous anti-discrimination laws? The answer is probably "all of the above."

Or does the definition of essential diversity depend on the specific organizational context (age, location, scale, range of programs, etc.)? For this essay, and for the larger political discussion, clarity isn't needed. Appropriate representation means appropriate representation, universal and idiosyncratic at the same time. The value proposition is unassailable. Ask any foundation, any politician, or even some government agencies.

But there is at least one exception to this "universal" proposition which I want to explain if not defend. Boards of non-profit organizations play very different roles once one gets beyond the critically important mandatory legal (primarily fiduciary) functions. Board roles must be transparently clarified and defined and hierarchically valued. For those organizations where the primary role is fundraising from private resources, or access to the power-structure of either the government or private sector, representation may become a slightly less important goal. Representation and fundraising capabilities are not mutually exclusive, and certainly there are enough real-time examples to prove that point. But "enough" is not a lot, and not so easily achieved. If only! Most boards look for members who look like them. This is neither right nor helpful, and can be self-defeating in achieving important goals, but is a phenomenon difficult to overcome.

Every Board wants to be and do everything. They want to exemplify all relevant criteria. They want to provide the resources and influence needed for success. In the non-profit sector, however, exceptions prove the rule. Diversity is the vision; it may not be the path to organizational strength and sustainability.

(Note: The "exception" I describe here should rarely apply to the rules which govern staff hiring and retention. For many organizations, the "time dimension," applicable human resource protocols, union requirements, or even the specific job requirements may prevent the effective implementation of a policy to have staff represent the issues and communities served by the organization. In my experience, however, this self-evident value and goal is easier to achieve if not directly tied to the roles and responsibilities assigned to the Board of Directors.

Fighting with Friends

What could be worse than having to challenge the decisions or strategies of your friends when they assume positions of authority, influence, or power which may negatively affect your organizational obligations and the lives of people you are committed serve? Advocacy is always easier when the personal and professional boundaries and goals are different for the involved players, when the other side is unmistakable, when the battle lines are unambiguous. Inevitably, however, advocacy is needed even more when friends don't agree on specific and important matters when means and ends are in conflict. Advocacy is to argue for, and to argue against.

Unfortunately, any form of confrontation amongst friends is not just unpleasant and anxiety provoking. It can also be professionally damaging, psychologically exhausting, and long lasting in its negative impact. Conflict among friends is unexpected, creates new ground rules, makes you question who you are and what you're doing. **When advocating is what you need to do to fulfill your organizational mission, then advocacy is what you must**

do, irrespective of the personal consequences. The bonds of friendship must allow for and acknowledge this reality.

Hopefully, time will heal all wounds between folks on different sides of almost any issue. Such is the hoped-for nature of friendship, and frequently of deeper relationships. Presumably, there will be winners and losers in these fights, and one learns to accept wins and losses in equal measure. No one is happy about everything. The obligation of friends who fight over important issues is to understand the difference between the ground rules for friendship and the ground rules for doing your job. And since, over time, many of us get to play multiple roles, placing us on different sides of some issues, some longitudinal perspective helps.

It is generally accepted by non-profit practitioners as a truism that when a person moves from this sector to a responsible government position, it takes only moments for that person to forget all the realities of non-profit management and to become a strong advocate of, or convert to, the new job/administration one is representing. An equal and opposite truism is that when a government sector person takes a nonprofit management or leadership position, any decision or policy implemented in the former position was not of your doing. Therefore, you can no longer be held accountable. In both movements, one gets to say, "who me"? These realties are healthy, from one perspective, and movement between sectors is frequently a good thing. Forgetting one's previous life is both allowable and occasionally amusing. My advice on this issue? Recognize the importance of personal and professional memory and history. Each one of us gets to play multiple roles in our life, but it remains a single life. **Both the non-profit and government sectors would be better off if there was no necessity to forget one's past, that one can be an interesting**

combination of personas, worshipping both masters, even if only one is paying you at the time. Memory and respect should be seen as virtues on both sides.

A related, and somewhat frustrating phenomenon, is when nonprofit advocates publicly agree on a course of action, and privately pursue their own interests which may conflict with the communal public stance. No one should be surprised when this happens, but there is an implicit assumption among "social justice" folks that we should collaborate when collaboration is the path to better outcomes. Communal action denies, however, one of the guiding principles of organizational behavior: self-preservation. In the end, nonprofit organizations think about their own sustainability, survival, short and longer-term success. Developing and defending a corporate strategy which defends private interests while simultaneously supporting communal interests calls for talents not widely available in management circles.

Empathy Is Outdated

An organization driven solely by empathetic values is no longer sustainable. At the same time, an organization which buries the power of empathy needs to be dissolved. An individual leader who makes decisions allowing empathy to be a guiding influence is doomed to fail. An individual leader who fails to understand the value of empathy in making decisions is equally doomed to fail. **Balancing empathy with fulfilling one's professional obligations is the essence of wisdom.** If there is anything in the political universe which I never seem to understand, it is the cruelty to others either implicit or explicit in peoples' actions and decisions. No advice here.

The Fallacy of Dashboards and Other Tools

If only the world was knowable, logical, rational, capable of being measured and organized in "dashboards" (aka key performance indicators, "KPIs"), or some other acronyms I can't remember. But such tools of management, whatever their value, are not the same as what it takes to be a strong and effective leader. We should have learned this principle back when the "limits of rationality" arguments were being argued and resolved, when every step in any definition of the rational strategic planning model was simultaneously defended and debunked. "Muddling through," "disjointed incrementalism," "satisficing," and so many other terms were applied to the realities of strategic thinking and decision making. The best managers were those who understood the glories and weaknesses of rationality, the limits of information and knowing everything you need to know when making decisions, and the conflicting dynamics of facts and values.

We must remember some principles of limited rationality:

> organizations cannot easily plan for the future because the future is too uncertain;

> even if an organization has a plan, it is not always prudent to publically acknowledge it exists;

> organizations rarely consider fundamentally different alternatives;

> organizations prefer present rather than future value and effects (the future is discounted);

organizational maintenance is usually more important than any other end;

people have limited problem solving capacities;

information is always incomplete and inadequate;

analysis is costly;

evaluation systems are costly and frequently inaccurate;

separating facts from values is not so easy;

systems tend to be open, not closed, making analysis fluid and imprecise; and so on.

This list never gets shorter. The words, or ordering of words, change with every new writer and each generation.

Advances in communications and technologies have not changed the nature of organizations…or leaders. More information presented in more accessible formats is certainly better for organizational performance, and benefits all stakeholders – including staff, Boards, and external players. The value of effective informational tools should be obvious, especially in an era when reading anything with complex sentence structure or multiple paragraphs is passé. However, information, and the tools to communicate that information, are not sufficient for organizational success. New managerial language may be fascinating, but it is fleeting. If not connected to organizational performance.

Why No One Writes About (Having Good) Judgment

The very nature of management and leadership is predicated on making judgments. The processes of successfully running an organization and the processes of making judgments are so similar conceptually that we might constructively question if and where the boundaries exist between the two. To make a judgment call is to reach a decision, to state a position, to assert or be identified with a particular stance, to select or choose from among alternatives, to think in a particular fashion. Judgment is not the same as action though it may require action to assert its value over time. Judgment is explicitly married to strategic decision making, which is what leaders do.

And yet we rarely talk about people having good JUDGMENT when we assess performance, perhaps reflecting the subjective or situational nature of the concept. We use words like smart, intelligent, even wise....and each has its value. Dissecting the nuanced differences among these terms may be a useful exercise for someone other than me. Now is the time, however, to get over this hesitation to avoid using judgment as a measure of effective leadership. In the end, having good judgment may be the only thing that counts.

From my perspective, judgment requires the integration of several qualities:

(1) having sufficient substantive/technical knowledge to understand the subject area to which the judgment relates;

(2) having knowledge and understanding of the historical context in which the judgment is to be made;

(3) having an imagination, the ability to creatively interpret or envision the past, present and future, the ability to deal with abstractions and concrete realities at the same time;

(4) having a personal value framework that influences the ways in which the world is perceived and evaluated;

(5) having an awareness of how action (implementation) will affect the judgment that is being expressed (i.e. anticipatory reality testing).

That this process is subjective is obvious; nonetheless, judgment for leaders is tied to things real and solid. Judgments may be idiosyncratic, potentially inconsistent, primarily tacit, but they are what we are measured by, or should be measured by. The power of judgment is to understand that people make judgments all the time. Judgments are subject to the nuances of time, can be identified and considered on either a specific or more abstract basis, and are inextricably linked to public review, assessment, praise or condemnation.

Endnotes

As a nonprofit manager, I had no need to connect with the world of book publication, so when I decided to write this collection of essays, I was on my own. I also managed to skip having an editor, publicist, or agent, both by choice and not understanding the process. When I needed feedback or advice or encouragement, I turned to friends who would be honest but reasonably gentle.

In the end, I owe thanks to a small group who took the time to read a few or all of the essays in this collection. My most important reader was Bob Howitt, a friend now for many years and the person who first got me involved with The Door. He read every paragraph in every essay, making substantive recommendations as well as an infinite number of grammatical corrections or suggestions. Our many breakfasts together ensured that I would finish this project. Stephan Russo, my fellow settlement house leader and friend, had suggestions on every essay, but more importantly reinforced the basic motivations for my writing, i.e. practitioners need to write about their experiences and insights.

Jeff Scheuer, who wrote The Legacy of Light, the history of University Settlement, always reminded me that writing is a labor of love. Nancy Wackstein, a friend and settlement house peer, encouraged me to fight for the needed connections between the worlds of service and educational introspection. Peter Pullman edited a few of the essays, with both honesty and amazing perception. Many other friends and associates read pieces of the collection, responded to my ideas, argued with my conclusions, encouraged me to publish the essays, and promised to buy millions of copies if this was ever published.

Special thanks to Amanda Peck who nurtured my first book into a reality, and now has done the same for this collection of essays. She possesses insights and talents which have made my work more accessible than it deserves.

The essays are designed as reflections of a personal story, my story.

I began the collection with reference to my first grandchild, Caleb. I now have a second grandchild, Lila. My family has always come first for me, as all my personal and professional friends have always understood. My grandchildren, my wife Marsha, my daughters Emma and Margaret, my sons-in-law Jason and Corey, are "why I do this."

Michael Zisser

Fall 2018

CPSIA information can be obtained
at www.ICGtesting.com
Printed in the USA
BVHW071327160119
537964BV00005B/603/P